ROTAS, RULES AND RECTORS

ROTAS, RULES
AND
RECTORS

How to thrive being
a Churchwarden

MATTHEW CLEMENTS

Matador
9 Priory Business Park,
Wistow Road, Kibworth Beauchamp,
Leicestershire. LE8 0RX
Tel: 0116 279 2299
Email: books@troubador.co.uk
Web: www.troubador.co.uk/matador
Twitter: @matadorbooks

ISBN 978 1789016 314

British Library Cataloguing in Publication Data.
A catalogue record for this book is available from the British Library.

Printed and bound in Great Britain by 4edge Limited
Typeset in 11pt Bembo by Troubador Publishing Ltd, Leicester, UK

Matador is an imprint of Troubador Publishing Ltd

Dedicated to the many friends and fellow workers
who have, over the years, unwittingly provided
much of the material for this book.

Table of Contents

Foreword

Churchwardens are the great unsung heroes of the Church of England. If you are reading this book, you are probably aware of that, either being a churchwarden yourself, or considering the possibility of becoming one, or working alongside one. Matthew Clements is far too much of a Christian to proclaim his own virtues, but the great strength of his writing is that he sets the sometimes dry duties and responsibilities of wardenship within the warm context of human lives lived joyously and devotedly in the service of Christ and his beloved Church.

I was privileged to serve as archdeacon for a number of years alongside the author and entirely recognise the truth of his wife's comment that he was "born to be a churchwarden". That remains the case for surprisingly many wardens in the Church of England today; some others achieve this office after years of waiting, and a great many have it thrust upon them. Whatever the route by which God calls them into this role, though, all should be honoured for the greatness of the task they have taken up; and all will find in this book practical wisdom, shrewd common sense and indefatigable commitment to a noble cause.

Rt Revd Dr Michael Ipgrave OBE
Bishop of Lichfield

Preface

If you have recently been elected as a Churchwarden (CW) – this book is for you; congratulations on being brave enough to put your head above the parapet. If you are thinking of accepting nomination as CW, then it's for you too. I hope that I can persuade you that the job is worth doing and that this book might help you to do it better, enjoy it more and thrive in it! Even if you have been a CW for some time, I hope that you will find some useful tips here as well as some good examples of what can happen.

Perhaps you are a member of a Parochial Church Council (PCC) and want to understand why your CWs are sometimes a bit tired and irritable; or are you thinking of nominating someone for the role of CW and wonder if they can do it? I hope that this book will give you enough to think about and help you answer that question. You might even want to give them a copy – or volunteer yourself.

On the other hand, you might be a vicar somewhere wondering how best to use your CWs or what sort of person you should look for as a CW. You might even have had a poor experience with a few in your career – don't necessarily blame yourself! I hope that this book will tell you what sort of job your CWs should do and what you should be able to expect from them; you too might even want to give a copy of the book to the lucky people who get voted as CWs at the next APCM.

There are other published books which give all sorts of detail about the legalities of PCC meetings and elections. These books are very useful, and you will want to buy at least one, to take with you to meetings such as the PCC or the Annual Meeting where you can adjudicate on how many members make a meeting quorate, or how many ex-officio members a PCC can have. This book isn't like that – it's aimed rather at detailing some of the practical responsibilities of the job and giving a flavour of what it involves, based on my own experiences over twenty-four years as CW (twice) and treasurer (once), all in different parishes and dioceses, as well as previously being CW for a short time at one church on an RAF station.

People often ask what the difference is between a rector and a vicar. The simple answer is "patronage", which only matters when you are choosing a new one, and the reason for this is largely historical. Hence, for simplicity in the text I will just use the term "vicar" to mean either vicar or rector.

Obviously, in this day and age, both men and women can be a vicar, archdeacon or bishop and, naturally, both men and women can also be CWs (I wonder when the first woman CW was elected). However, in the interests of balance and anonymity, I have randomly allocated the gender to any person. If I used "s/he" then I would also have to use "him/her" and "his/hers" and then the whole thing is a bit unwieldy. I will refer to "the CW" when quite often I should refer to "the CWs", so please interpret that term to mean both CWs in a church, where appropriate.

I am sure that many friends will recognise the places and may therefore recognise themselves. I will therefore apologise in advance to those who might recognise themselves or their friends in any particular story that I might tell; no personal offence is intended and I can only also say "thank you" to them for providing such useful anecdotes for this book!

1

Churchwarden – Me?

You might be wondering why you allowed yourself to be proposed or elected as churchwarden. Perhaps you are still considering whether to accept this nomination and wonder what you have to offer. Well, this book is intended to help you understand what is involved in the job – be aware that it is neither an honorary position nor a sinecure – and to give you sufficient direction for you to be able to do your best in this role, whilst also enjoying it.

You might be thinking that you cannot possibly do the job and that there is no way you will allow yourself to be pushed into doing it as you don't have the knowledge, experience or confidence. You might not be able to tell a mullion from a merlon, but you don't really need to know that – you pick that sort of thing up as you go! You might be thinking that you will be succeeding a well-organised individual who has done the job for years and made it look easy and unstressed – *How could I step in his shoes? He works so hard.* On the other hand, your predecessor might appear to have been lazy, weak, uninterested, arrogant or casual, which might have made you think that you could do the job better – *What does she do with her time? There's nothing to that job, is there? If he can do it then it can't be that difficult! I wouldn't do the job that way.* Whatever your perceptions are of CWs, the odds are that the job they do has little in common with your understanding of what it entails!

A CW obviously has responsibilities in church services, and people see these (and notice the mistakes!). The congregation will always have expectations of what should be done in any church, and how it should be done; moreover, different congregations (e.g., at baptisms, funerals and civic services) will have very different expectations to the usual Sunday congregation. The visible part of the CW job in a service of any sort is to ensure that those particular expectations are met. In a way, the CW can be regarded as the "front of house manager", whose major role is to ensure that the "customers" have the experience that they expect from the "performance". I will discuss this most important aspect later. CWs also have an occasional ceremonial role which has gently reduced over the years; again this is seen and acknowledged by the congregation and, at times, by the general public.

However, there is more to the job than the services; even "Rotas, Rules and Rector" only illustrates a small part of the task, as a very large proportion of the CW job is hidden from most people in the church – it is the "behind the scenes" work of a "stage manager" rather than just "front of house"; they might see and even appreciate the end result, but the effort involved in achieving it will largely pass unnoticed. There are meetings to attend, decisions to be made, emails to reply to, information to be passed on, people to badger (sorry, I mean "volunteers to find

2

and rotas to fill"), faculties to be prepared, contractors to manage. All of these things must be done by someone, and that someone is very often the CW. If it is not the CW, then quite possibly she will have been instrumental in asking someone else to do it.

It is probably true that I have not fully appreciated the work of my various predecessors as CW. They will have done the job in their way and will have been subject to different pressures, for instance, due to different vicars, a different financial situation and a different public perception. I can only judge them by what I see of their work now, and I am painfully aware that those in the future will judge me by the same light. The answer to this is to ignore it – others did and will do the job in their own way, and you should do it in your own way. All I give here is guidance based on my experience and the way that I chose to do the job; you might well get great results by doing it in a completely different way. I just hope that I can stimulate your thinking to approach the job with enthusiasm and a proactive aim, rather than just drift passively through your time as CW.

I'm a Chartered Engineer by profession, and so you might guess that I am a quite logical person. I like to see things work properly, according to the design and process, so the metaphor I like for the CW job is a mechanical one. I liken the job to being the oil in a car engine which lubricates all the moving parts. By so doing, it reduces friction between various components which move at different speeds. It is hard to have too much oil around these components, but you will certainly notice the effect when you don't have enough!

Try running your car engine without any oil in it; initially, you might not notice any difference apart from a warning light illuminating. That first light will probably be orange, but in my car if you ignore the first warning then soon a red light will come on with some worrying symbol which you don't comprehend. You ignore that one at your peril! If you do, before long, everything will get very heated and things will not work properly; metal-to-metal contact will make parts wear out rapidly, the maximum power will be reduced and loud protesting noises will emanate from the engine. Ultimately, the engine will stop, seized solid, never to restart; now you wish you had understood what the warning signs were telling you! The car manufacturer will tell you in the vehicle handbook what sort of oil you should use. Then, if you make sure that you have sufficient oil of the right type in your engine, you will never really appreciate its presence. It's there and it just does the job, quietly and continuously, day in, day out, with the occasional oil change at the recommended intervals. You might know a CW who is like that, and if so then I strongly suggest that you hang on to her! Sadly, however, I have known some who seemed to have added sand or metal particles to their oil; everything sounded and felt a bit scratchy, and people around them got worn out with the constant friction. In other cases, the oil wasn't changed when it should have been, and the old oil has ceased to do its job properly.

When I was a teenager, the post of the CW was a revered and highly respected one. To me then it appeared to be a bit like the mayor of our town council – a sort of ceremonial appointment which was shared around by those who were also waiting for their turn in a few years. In fact, at that time, even to be on the PCC was a sought-after position, with a contested election each year. Sadly, those days are long gone and many PCCs struggle to fill posts with "volunteers" of any calibre; we are far away from the days of being able to choose which candidate to elect as the best of several well-qualified nominees.

However, looking back, I realise that in fact I had absolutely no idea of what those CWs did then, apart from process around during certain services clutching their staves. Perhaps they weren't actually that busy. Somehow, I think that was not the case; and I apologise to the departed for not fully appreciating their hard work at the time.

2

Born To Be A
Churchwarden?

I do not believe that you have to be born to be a churchwarden, as I maintain that the CW job can be done by almost anyone. You just need a modicum of intelligence and organisation, coupled with the ability to delegate and the confidence to make a few decisions; possibly a decent amount of patience and perseverance would help as well because you will be criticised and loaded with tasks. In other words, there is nothing technically taxing in the job, but really it's all about how you approach it and how you get on with people.

However, a few years ago, my wife was the subject of the back page interview in *Church Times*. One paragraph of that is usually devoted to the interviewee's family, and there she made a memorable comment: *My husband was born to be a churchwarden!* Whilst I think that this is a remarkable overstatement of my abilities, I do accept that it does perhaps give some indication of my calling to the task.

How I first became a Church Officer

In the early years of our marriage, we as a couple were a bit variable in our choice of church to attend. Despite meeting in our teens at an evangelical Anglican church, our choice on setting up home together in a new town was Baptist. Mind you, that choice was partly determined by the two local Anglican churches: one had a sign outside saying "Confessions by arrangement", and so we tried the other. At that church, the curate spoke to us before the service and asked us if we would like to join the choir, which seemed a bit premature; when the choir processed in, we saw there were more people in the choir than in the congregation! Consequently, the following week we tried the local Baptist church where we were welcomed warmly. A couple of years later, I joined the Royal Air Force; at the typical RAF station there is a choice of three churches: the Roman Catholics, the Anglicans and the "Church of Scotland and Free Churches" (CSFC), i.e., "the rest". We were never worried about seeking a welcome in the CSFC if it seemed the right choice.

At one station, I had my first taste of being CW. I had been there only a few weeks when I was asked if I would fill the vacant second post – there were no elections then, as you never stayed long enough! One week after I accepted, the existing CW announced that he was giving up the job – clearly, he had been waiting for the arrival of just such a person to end his own time of responsibility. Almost two years later, still the sole CW, I was posted, leaving someone else to pick up the mantle. We had quickly become used to this in the RAF – you find your roles and make friends quickly and then leave at the same sort of speed a couple of years later. We lived in five locations in my first ten years in the RAF before getting some stability at the sixth. That place was different as, unusually, there was no church at all on the RAF station, and so we were forced to try elsewhere. Initially, we went to the village church, just a pleasant walk down the high street; however, I recall the dusty atmosphere, the lack of welcome and the vicar trying to teach the congregation a chorus (possibly "*Wide, wide as the ocean*") which we had learned many years before as teenagers (anyone remember the red book of CSSM choruses?); this didn't feel like our sort of place, so again we tried a Baptist church, some miles away, where we as a family were welcomed with open arms.

After three years with the Baptists, we both separately felt that we should leave. On my part, this was due to a feeling of having become ill at ease in most church activities. The obvious place to try again was the same local Anglican church, where the atmosphere seemed to have improved compared to our earlier visit, and we stayed for thirteen happy years, during which time I left the RAF. (To protect the innocent, I will call this "Anchorton Church", and I will also say that it is in the "Diocese of Anchorton" and has a "Vicar of Anchorton", etc.)

We became heavily involved in Anchorton Church where somehow (to my surprise) I became in charge of the Sunday School. I am not a trained teacher and that role didn't come easily to me, so after several years I worked out my exit strategy by becoming church treasurer, a job that I felt qualified for by virtue of having just gained an MBA qualification. After my appointment as treasurer, the vicar asked me if I was going to "keep an eye" on the Sunday School and he was then a bit shocked when I said "no", as I considered I had left behind a good team who knew what they were doing. I did the treasurer job for five years, which included a couple of years whilst my wife was CW. Also, for most of that time, I was concurrently the treasurer of a small registered charity and also, for a short spell, Deanery treasurer as well. In those five years, I saw the introduction of three major changes:

- The introduction of Gift Aid rules (replacing the old covenant system)
- The new Church Accounting Rules (when there had been effectively none)
- The use of a computer (instead of handwritten double entry accounting ledgers, as I got very bored with entering over forty standing orders each month, and I made numerous mistakes)

If you understand the job of a church treasurer then you will realise just how monumental all three of those changes were, and how much hard work they entailed.

Experience as a Churchwarden

We moved to Bogthornly after thirteen years so that we could both be closer to our new jobs. We felt that the move was right, despite some respected and well-intentioned people at Anchorton saying that they were praying that we would change our minds! I became CW at Bogthornly in less than two years and, due to my knowledge and experience, had a good input into finances as well. That church was centuries old but had been completely rebuilt at least once, and that was my first experience of working on a listed building. In fact, I amused several people (including the Archdeacon) by paying for myself to go on a one-day course called "An Introduction to Lime Mortar" which has proved most beneficial to my work with old churches, not to mention our current house. I would add that the move to Bogthornly is a great example of the fact that God has a sense of humour: two years before moving from Anchorton, I can recall saying publicly that we were thinking of moving somewhere – 'anywhere but an inner-city church' and so a multiracial inner-city church was exactly where we found ourselves two years later, and we enjoyed it immensely. I made many friends from a wide variety of backgrounds with which I would not normally have had much contact – people living in genuine poverty, disadvantaged people, single-parent families and many so poor that they did not have bank accounts. It was here that I realised just how privileged my upbringing was, and how many things I had which I simply took for granted.

After seven years at Bogthornly, I was made redundant from my job and took early retirement, moving to Clamcester (a growing town in the countryside) where we still live. I have just finished my sixth and last year as CW at Clamcester where, again, I have had a good hand in the finances. In my time as CW we have completed four major conservation and renovation projects on the church, not to mention several smaller projects. I am still heavily involved in the maintenance of two listed buildings – the church and our house across the road (which needed months' of work before my wife and I could even move in).

I do believe that God guides me quite clearly in all the major decisions of life, from the surprising job which I was given out of the blue when I left the RAF, to the call to leave the city and move to the countryside, to the house where we now live and the church where we worship. In all these, I have been conscious of hearing His unmistakeable voice. Just as happened at Bogthornly, I became CW at Clamcester within less than two years; I wasn't really surprised by the appointment, just the speed.

So you can see why perhaps yes, I was indeed born to be a CW, though perhaps not quite in the sense that my wife meant in her interview. Rather, I was born to be the CW here, using my God-given skills and knowledge to further the work of His church in this place.

You must have a story to tell as well. It is your story, and of course it is different to mine. I have related mine just as an illustration of the fact that God calls us and equips us to do work for Him. Sometimes it is work for which we are well suited with training and experience; but sometimes that call might be a total surprise, to something for which you feel you have no training or experience. You might not think that you are born to be a CW, but you might be called to do it, and your response to that call is the important thing.

3

Just What Does A Churchwarden Do?

The Legal Duties of a Churchwarden

The role of the churchwarden (CW) is an ancient one, older than the role of the police, for example. Given the passage of time, you could be forgiven for assuming that the responsibilities of the CWs would be clearly set out, and that somewhere there is a comprehensive list which tells you just what a CW has to do. One feels that there should be something to ring-fence the apparently ever-increasing scope of this job, surely?

Wrong; there isn't. If in doubt about where the responsibility lies, there is no doubt: it falls to the CW. Basically, in general, I would say that the CW is ultimately responsible for almost everything in a church that does not need to be done by the vicar. If the CW doesn't do it, then she is responsible for making sure that it gets done by someone (and that can include things often done by vicars!).

Of course, there are lots of things that the CW should never need to be bothered with: the bell-ringers, flower arrangers, Mothers' Union, choir, youth work, etc… But the point is that if there is any issue or problem in any area, then the CW needs to hear about it and needs to judge when to get involved. If you have a strong team at a large church, you should be able to rely on most of these things happening regardless, being done by people who know what they are doing and like doing it; at a smaller church with fewer volunteers, you might even be doing many of these things yourself already, and then an important part of the CW job will be to encourage new volunteers.

I frequently think that most members of the PCC and congregation do not appreciate how much work the CWs do, how much time it takes, what goes on behind the scenes and how much pressure there is. There might even be some people who like to make jokes in your direction "because you like being busy". All that these people see is the public side of the job and they assume that it's a complete doddle. I would say that it isn't that simple, but I wouldn't want to discourage you from grasping this nettle. It is rewarding when you get it right, even if people don't necessarily thank you.

My view has always been that as CW, I should be helping the vicar to do her job more effectively, by taking away from her as many as possible of the tasks that she doesn't need to do personally. The trouble is, some vicars are control freaks and don't like to relinquish control in the slightest – I think they see their job as power and, of course, control equals power. Nevertheless, I persist in my view and still try to shield my vicar from jobs that can be done by anyone else (even though that probably means me in many cases). I don't lead services, visit the sick or preach, but if I can help the vicar to do activities like those more effectively, by me doing more of something boring or ordinary, then I think I am playing my part in the Kingdom.

The law about the CW role, as such, is in just three places:

- Church of England Canon E1
- The Churchwardens Measure 2001
- Ecclesiastical Courts Jurisdiction Act 1860

All of these are available online via a search engine and are worth a look. The Church of England website has all the canons (which deserve a general read), and the other two are at legislation.gov.uk, which is a site worth knowing. If you know the title or general subject of any Act of Parliament (and that includes the General Synod of the C of E) then you should be able to find the actual wording there. You might need to read the Measure through several times before you will be able to understand what it is telling you, as it was written by lawyers for lawyers.

Conversely, the first of these sources, Canon E1, is remarkable in its simplicity: *The churchwardens when admitted are officers of the bishop. They shall discharge such duties as are by law and custom assigned to them; they shall be foremost in representing the laity and in co-operating with the incumbent; they shall use their best endeavours by example and precept to encourage the parishioners in the practice of true religion and to promote unity and peace among them. They shall also maintain order and decency in the church and churchyard, especially during the time of divine service.*

There are a few more words but essentially that's all it says. No explanations, no definitions, no detail. It's not much to go on, is it? But saying so much in so few words could actually be seen as a good thing, as it gives flexibility and discretion.

Being *an officer of the bishop* means, inter alia, that the CW has direct access to the bishop. Moreover, it is the CW's DUTY to speak to the bishop ABOUT the vicar if necessary. The Church of England is not a truly hierarchical organisation, despite what people might think. The CWs have the right to bypass the vicar and go further up the line to the bishop (probably via the Area Dean or Archdeacon first) if the situation warrants. Hopefully, this does not happen often for many CWs, but it is an important right and duty which should not be forgotten if the priest ever oversteps the mark in any legal or spiritual way. Sadly, this sort of thing does happen, and the CWs then need to discern when an approach to the bishop should be made.

They shall discharge such duties as are by law and custom assigned to them. That's pretty general, isn't it? You might not know the law, but probably you do know the local customs. Of course, the customs should not be against the law, but rather they should amplify the law in a manner that is acceptable locally. Equally, there is nothing to stop you from adding to these local customs if you so choose, but bear in mind that customs need a valid reason; search online for the *Story of the Cat and the Monks* and you will see what I mean. Conversely, you could well find that there are some things that need to be done but no one is doing them. You have a choice – do them yourself or find someone who will do them, because the custom will probably be that the responsibility falls to the CWs!

They shall be foremost in representing the laity and in co-operating with the incumbent. The CWs should act as a focal point for the laity who might well find it easier to speak to the CWs about an issue or concern than to ask the vicar; hence it is important that the CWs are approachable by being known and respected. Conversely, the CWs should maintain a good relationship with the vicar so that the flow of information is also in the opposite direction, towards the laity. I know that sounds as though the CWs might have to face two ways at the same time but, as I have said already, the job isn't always easy!

In the same way, *they shall use their best endeavours by example and precept to encourage the parishioners in the practice of true religion and to promote unity and peace among them.* So don't take sides, and don't encourage gossip or talking behind people's backs; I have found that a simple 'I don't like to talk about that sort of thing' usually successfully discourages people from repeating gossip, although at times physically turning away from such a conversation has been the only course open to me. Promoting "unity and peace" is not easy to do all the time, but the fruit is worth working for. Paradoxically, you have to be on everyone's side but also on no one's side, at the same time.

They shall also maintain order and decency in the church and churchyard, especially during the time of divine service. One hopes that this sort of responsibility will never need to be exercised, but I once had to go outside to the churchyard during a service to stop a group of council contractors who thought they could come back on a Sunday morning to trim the trees with a noisy chainsaw! Another time, on Remembrance Sunday, a very close neighbour decided to start using a sledgehammer to demolish a wall in his garden just outside the vestry, three minutes before the one minute's silence.

Secondly, the Churchwardens Measure 2001 is entirely about the election of CWs, not about their function. One important thing to note is that CWs are not elected at the APCM but at the annual "Parish Meeting" (also called the "Meeting of Parishioners"). This is because anyone resident in the parish (and on the register of local government electors) is able to vote for CWs, not just those on the electoral roll of the church. Of course, most churches will hold these two meetings sequentially on the same day; but legally, they are two separate meetings due to the different qualification for voters and should be kept distinct. Be careful, though, as most people will talk about the "APCM" when they mean either or both of these meetings.

Another point to note here is that some churches still make a distinction between the "Vicar's Warden" and the "People's Warden". This concept has been superseded, so these named roles no longer exist officially but are still used occasionally. This was an old way of doing things which might imply some disagreement between factions; I presume it was designed in order that the vicar knew he had one warden on his side, whilst keeping the people happy with a choice of their own. Nowadays, the Churchwardens Measure 2001 Section 4(5) has a way of dealing with a situation where there may be conflict anticipated between the vicar and a CW-designate. However, this being the C of E, I do not doubt that in 100 years' time there will still be a church somewhere that insists on using these terms, which by then will have acquired the status of a local quirky custom, its origins lost in the mists of time.

The third point above is an odd one. The Ecclesiastical Courts Jurisdiction Act 1860 is actually the law which, under certain conditions and circumstances, gives CWs the power of arrest! However, before you get your handcuffs out and polish them in anticipation, this is NOT recommended. The story goes that someone in a church or churchyard was behaving in a "riotous, violent, or indecent" fashion and one CW arrested them using the powers of this Act. However, when the police arrived, they arrested the unfortunate CW for "unlawful detention" or something similar; he then made a call to the diocesan registrar who had to educate the police regarding a law of which they had never heard. Eventually, the unfortunate CW was released from custody. This story was told by one Diocesan Registrar to the assembled CWs at a Visitation to make the point that just because you might have a legal right, you don't necessarily want to use that right. What you should do is call the police and tell them the specifics of the law so that THEY can make the arrest, if the circumstances warrant it.

Other Rules and Legalities

One of the books a CW needs is called the *Church Representation Rules.* It's a slim volume published by Church House Publishing which details the rules for election of officers and conduct of PCC meetings and the APCM. Knowledge of this stuff is invaluable – you don't need to know these rules by heart; you just need to know how to use the helpful index to find what you want in about one hundred pages.

However, that's about as far as it goes. So long as elections and meetings are conducted within the rules, and so long as an annual report is produced as specified (see later), then the legal requirements of the job are being done.

However, the unspecified scope for a CW is vast, and you have a choice: you can either follow the rules and ignore everything else, or you can take charge and see where it takes you. I'd like to be able to point you to some additional authoritative source of the other legal aspects of the CW's responsibilities but, sadly, I can't. In many ways, though, I think this is a good thing. As soon as you start becoming rule-bound, you lose flexibility, and I consider flexibility to be highly beneficial – it gives you scope for discretion and the use of your own intelligence, rather than simply following a binding set of prescribed rules.

Let me give you an example: when I was in the Royal Air Force as an engineer officer, I had the same choice about rules or discretion, and it certainly was not in my nature to allow myself to be constrained by rules if there was some doubt or flexibility about them. I regarded those areas of doubt as the opportunity to use my intelligence, training and experience to interpret the rules and so demonstrate my acceptance of responsibility because that was how the job was meant to be. I believe that it is times like that when the real satisfaction in doing a job is found, because I could go home on those days knowing that I had made a positive contribution rather than having taken the easy route. Life is not black and white – there are shades of grey wherever you look. Moreover, if you expect to find rules which will govern precisely what you need to do in life, then you will surely be disappointed.

As CW, you have this almost undefined broad responsibility, and I encourage you to display the authority that accompanies it; therefore, I strongly advise you to know and understand the rules (such as they are), so that you can make your own decisions, after taking advice when necessary. The job doesn't have a clear job specification, nor does it have clearly stated objectives, but the scope is very wide, so I earnestly recommend that you take hold of the challenge and make it your own. Passing the buck is all very well, but it doesn't give the satisfaction of a job well done. I think it also leads to people bypassing you, as next time they will go straight to the person to whom you passed the buck on the first occasion. There is nothing that will stop you, if you so choose, from being a nominal CW who allows everything to flow around him, apart from your own attitude; however, I don't think that you will find the job very satisfying. If you start off at the outset thinking positively about your responsibilities, it is much easier to delegate them later; conversely, if you have passed the buck to start with, it will almost certainly prove much more difficult to take back control later.

One of the people who made most impact on my unpaid career in the C of E was a retired brigadier at Anchorton. He was a fixture at the Diocesan Synod and so had been ex-officio on the PCC for decades, it seemed. You might think he sounds a real stereotype – the retired brigadier who speaks with a plum in his mouth, straight out of an Agatha Christie whodunnit – but that is quite misleading. He was a man of faith who knew his stuff; he knew charity law, the rules for PCCs and APCMs and so on, and we always turned to him for a definitive statement on such matters. He knew his way around the diocese and he spoke with both logic and careful thought – it all gave him an air of authority at meetings which, added to his natural demeanour, made him quite a formidable character.

I learned a lot from him about the rules and these other matters. When I took over as treasurer he asked me to visit him at home in the village for a chat, so I walked round (fortunately). In his study he offered me a drink and then opened a cupboard under his desk, which to my surprise contained a fridge! He gave me a generous G&T, possibly a treble. An hour later, after much discussion and advice, he said, 'Would you like the other half?' and so I had another similarly huge G&T before staggering home, wiser in two ways!

When he died a few years ago, I realised that I was now filling that same role on the PCC at Clamcester. Effectively, I had become the "retired brigadier", although I was not even close to equalling that rank in the RAF. I might not remember all the legal details (especially so as the years pass), but I know where the rules are, and I am not afraid to point them out when appropriate or even, I admit, to use them to my advantage sometimes.

By the way, whilst in the RAF, I also learned another important principle of life: *never ask a question to which I might not want to know the answer.* Some senior officers seemed to be over-cautious, treading on eggshells the whole time, and so I knew that, if asked, they would err on the side of caution every time. By not asking them, at least I didn't give them the chance to forbid me from doing it, which might have made my problem worse. For example, one evening during the late 80s, a friend of mine was on his way to Belfast for a meeting when he heard that there had been an explosion near his destination. Whilst still in England, he rang HQ and asked for advice from the duty security person, who of course advised him not to complete his journey – what else was he going to say? – so the meeting had to be cancelled, although I had already landed in Belfast for that meeting. So I had to return to London the next day, having achieved precisely nothing in twenty-four hours apart from consuming two pints of Guinness, but I did get home hours before my friend! For me, the principle remains good even in church circles – know the rules and make your own decision.

Sometimes people think that the rules are some sort of pedant's charter, made for people like me to use to the annoyance of everyone else. What they forget is that the rules are there for a reason. For instance, there is a rule about joining the electoral roll. Although you can join at any time, if you want to vote at the APCM, you have to be on the roll at least fourteen days before the APCM. There is a reason for this: at the start of the APCM at Bogthornly, the vicar would stand up and ask, 'Is there anyone else who would like to be on the electoral roll?' I told him that he shouldn't do this, but he did it again the next year. I think he eventually understood when I explained it to him after the third year: the rule is there for his protection as it prevents a large group of parishioners arriving at the APCM without notice, all joining the electoral roll (as is their right) and then effectively taking over the meeting because they outvote all the regulars. I don't know for certain but I bet that somewhere once there was an APCM with only five or ten members present where it did happen.

Another misconception about the rules is that there are classes of membership of the PCC. There aren't. If you are a member of the PCC, whether ex-officio, co-opted or elected, you have one vote, the same as everyone else (although I must state for clarity that the secretary, if not elected or co-opted, is just a minute taker and so in that case is not a member of any sort). The only exception about voting is that the chair has a casting vote in the event of a tied vote, although personally I think that if a decision is that close then you should agree instead to look at the question more extensively at a subsequent meeting rather than moving forward at once in a probably divisive fashion.

At Clamcester, a paid lay worker was (correctly) ex-officio on the PCC, but he had the view that he could only vote on things that were to do with his ministry and that everything else was not his concern. In the same way, other co-opted members sometimes seem to think that they are lesser beings of some sort; a quasi-legal inferiority complex. However, in the eyes of the law, all PCC members are trustees of the charity and have equal status in law. This confers on them legal responsibilities of which they might not have been aware before their election! The Charity Commission (CC) has a good set of documents available online which detail such matters, and it is probably a good idea for candidates to be made aware of their responsibilities before their election rather than afterwards. Also, one of the requirements of the CC is that trustee details including date of birth and address are provided to them. Whilst these are not published on the CC website, I have known individuals refuse to give these details, as though I had asked for their online banking password! This refusal made the job of entering the data rather difficult, so I am now at pains to point out this requirement before the election.

One important rule that CWs must be aware of is the Churchwardens Measure 2001 Section 3 which sets their term of office at six years – yes, just SIX years, with a gap of at least two years before they can be re-elected. To my mind, this is pretty sensible as I feel that one can become tired and stale if you stay in any job for too long. However, for those who are masochistic, there is an option: the same section says that the Annual Parish Meeting *may by resolution decide that this section shall not apply*. So, if you want to serve for more than six years, then you need to discuss this at the PCC and get an appropriate resolution passed at the Annual Parish Meeting. However, be careful as, if that resolution suspends the rule indefinitely, you may have made a rod for your own back because you have just signed away your "Get Out Of Jail Free" card; make sure the suspension is for a limited period, only for as long as you might want to serve. Now, some sources say that this vote must be made by an Annual Parish Meeting prior to that election (i.e., before or at the end of the CW's fifth year), but that is actually not what the Measure says; it simply says that the meeting must pass such a resolution, which could therefore be done seconds before electing you for your seventh year as CW. If you want to ensure your exit and people think that the vote has to be made the year preceding, let them think that and don't point out the actual wording. Do you see what I meant above about "using my knowledge of the rules to my advantage"?

Another example of using the rules to my advantage was when we had a very large PCC, with several people who were basically passengers, and the elected members were fewer in number than the ex-officio and co-opted. One year, in order to reduce the size, I got the customarily co-opted treasurer and secretary to be elected instead so that they filled two of the vacancies, thereby reducing the size of the PCC by two. We also had one of our deanery synod members elected to the diocesan synod, and I deliberately failed to point out that we should therefore elect another member at the APCM to fill this vacancy on the deanery synod. Another member less!

You will appreciate that I am in favour of using the rules to my advantage where it is necessary, and it is amazing that few people ever show any interest in understanding them enough to actually have an argument about them. I mentioned that some vicars think that "control equals power", but I prefer to think that "knowledge equals power".

Characteristics of a Churchwarden

I would like to define the required characteristics of a CW and I have already mentioned some: a modicum of intelligence and organisation, the ability to delegate and make decisions (in modern terms, "management ability"), plus patience and perseverance. However, I really think it is almost impossible to be clearer because the requirement will change according to the type of church, its location, the vicar's personality, the congregation and a host of other influences.

In my view, the CW job is what you make it, and that will depend on how you mould your own character with the requirements. On one hand, you may be content to let things happen and let each person do what they want without reference to you, or at the other extreme you may want to control every single detail of every role in the church. The rules allow both cases, but I personally think that the best course is usually one somewhere between these two extremes. You need to know who can be relied upon, who needs advice or reassurance, who will blossom if given responsibility, or even who might have "wacky" views which could reflect badly on the church in some circumstances. You also need to learn when to get involved and when to stand back from a situation.

In my case, being a practical engineer who has restored an old house, it was inevitable that I should have a direct involvement in the practical maintenance of the church building – in fact, I was developing this role even before I became CW. However, I must stress that this detailed knowledge is not essential – you just need to be able to manage a maintenance plan to make sure that the important tasks are all done at the required periodicity by someone, but not necessarily yourself. (See the chapter on Maintenance for more details.) But there are other parts of the job mentioned in this book which can be done by almost anyone who has a decent amount of intelligence and the willingness to learn. There are also many routine parts of the job which every CW should have an interest in, but actually they often don't!

There are several further character traits of a CW which I should mention: he should be trustworthy, honest and beyond reproach. I made a decision whilst I was church treasurer at Anchorton that if anyone ever called into question my integrity then I would resign at once without argument. I have never even come close to doing that, apart from the time when a member of the congregation asked at the APCM whether it was right that the independent examiner (a member of the congregation) should do the job for so many years, implying that there was some sort of collusion between him and the treasurer! I kept the same principle in my mind when I became CW, and perhaps my mindset was apparent because such a topic was never even obliquely raised at any time.

St Paul said that he had become *all things to all people* so that he might save some (1 Corinthians 9:22, NRSV). In practical terms, that verse tells me that, as a Christian, I should get on with everyone and love them, but not necessarily agree with them. There are times (probably frequently!) when I have annoyed people and I have often said things that I regretted, sometimes even just seconds later. I know that I tend to let people know what I think before I have asked myself if actually saying so is helpful; I know I am not as wise as Solomon, nor as patient as Job, nor as loving as Christ. As CW, and especially during an interregnum, you too will be tested frequently by kind, loving people who neither acknowledge nor appreciate the amount of work that you do, and just do not understand the difficulties and pressures of the job.

4

The Archdeacon's Visitation

Every year the Archdeacon holds a Visitation which the CWs are obliged to attend. Well, actually the Archdeacon holds several and you are required to attend just one of them, not necessarily the nearest one if the date is inconvenient. The purpose of this event is for the "Admission of Churchwardens" by the Chancellor of the diocese, or else by the Registrar on his behalf. The ones I have attended have always been in the form of a service at which the Archdeacon preaches. The CWs are required to attend this ceremony/service every time that you are elected – your election is always for just a single year, so you are re-sworn each year.

For a newly elected CW, this is the legal moment at which you take over responsibility as CW, as the former CW is still in post until the new one is sworn in. Nevertheless, the rules anticipate such a delay, and the newly elected CW is by law a PCC member from the moment of election. Although you might have been elected weeks or even a couple of months earlier, this visitation is when your predecessor will actually hand you the keys (if he hasn't done so already), probably with a large smile at the same time, coupled with the air of a person who has just been released from jail.

I should say here that there is also a rule about ending as CW. If the Annual Parish Meeting fails to elect a successor for a CW, then that sitting CW remains in post until July 31st of that year, at which stage his tenure is automatically terminated and the other CW (if any) is fully responsible for everything. The sitting CW is not allowed to remain in post indefinitely because of a lack of a successor – he must be re-elected and then readmitted if he wants to serve for longer.

As an aside, you may sometimes encounter the term "Churchwarden Emeritus" or "Honorary Churchwarden". If you are honoured in this way after you complete your term, then please understand that it is a local honour and nothing more; the role has no legal standing whatsoever and does not confer a place on the PCC. I have heard of places where the "Churchwarden Emeritus" retained his place on PCC without being elected and continued to exert authority as a CW. This can only be detrimental to the position of his successor. The ex-CW should do all he can to assist his successor and not get in the way.

At this visitation service in both dioceses where I have been a CW, I have been given an envelope with a copious amount of paper which deserves attention. The most useful item in that pack is *Visitation News*, sponsored by Ecclesiastical Insurance. Half of this document is generic and the other half is specific to the diocese; last year it had some surprisingly interesting articles about the new faculty rules and new churchyard regulations. One other item was a small unpublished document entitled *A Guide to the Duties of a Churchwarden*, and this is the closest thing I have ever found to a concise summary of the CW duties, albeit not itself legally binding. The small print says *With thanks to the former Archdeacon of Charing Cross* (which is in a different diocese to any in which I have lived), so I guess he was the person who first produced this useful summary. I like the notes of caution such as: *The way in which CWs exercise their office will vary from parish to parish.* It's basically a helpful four-page A5 summary of a good part of this book, but having read this far you don't need to bother finding a copy!

Don't confuse this Visitation with the Archdeacon's Annual Inspection which is sometimes called a visitation as well and, even more confusingly, is often carried out by the Area Dean on her behalf; this is covered in a later chapter.

5

All The Same Team

The Other Churchwarden

Most churches have two elected churchwardens; there seems to be some local variation on this sort of thing, presumably for historical reasons – one CW friend of mine was certain that all churches were like his with just one CW, and I have been told of some with three for some historic reason. (I shall assume here that there are precisely two CWs, as that makes it easier, but most of these comments will still apply.) Sometimes there may be trouble in finding a volunteer and so a church may only have been able to elect one CW, and I even know of one church where have been none at all for three years! If there are the usual two, then you will always have an "other churchwarden", and equally from his point of view you are the "other churchwarden". This is likely to be a most important relationship for not just you both but also for the church. How you work together and, importantly, how you are seen to work together will have a major impact on the success of your tenure as CW.

Assuming that your church has two CWs, it makes sense that the first election for both is not the same year, if that can possibly be avoided. Of course you can do that if you really need to, but it seems to me that always having one who has been in the job a while will make life a lot easier for the new CW.

Now, as mentioned earlier, the legal maximum term for a CW is six years (the Churchwardens Measure 2001 Section 3, in case you had forgotten already) unless the Annual Parish Meeting approves otherwise. So if the CWs were always to do six years, then a new one would be elected every three years, which would mean that there is always one experienced CW in post, who can pass his hard-earned wisdom and knowledge on to the new CW. Of course, a lot of CWs will do less than six years, for all sorts of reasons. At Clamcester, it seemed that the expectation was to do only three years, but in my experience you have only just started to enjoy the job by then, so you should carry on and enjoy a few more years! Even if the CWs only do three or four years, you can surely manage the situation so that one has been in post for at least a year before the next new one comes along. In general, I suspect (for there are no statistics on this sort of thing) there are few contested CW elections, and CWs in post rarely lose out to a challenger; so the interesting thing is what happens when one decides to stand down at the next election?

"Manage the situation"? Yes, that's what I just said in the previous paragraph. You need to actively think about the Annual Parish Meeting and APCM well before that time comes along. If one CW is intending not to seek re-election, then a lot of thought and prayer has to go into this, a long time before the Annual Parish Meeting.

Although there is an election – and I would never wish to be accused of fixing an election – the best elections in a church are where there is no contest and the best candidates have been agreed already, with the right number of candidates for the right number of posts. I believe that it is best to get the two CWs proposed and seconded by the right people; thus if one is a new candidate, then a proposal for the new CW by the retiring CW, seconded by the other CW, is a good indicator to the rest of the congregation. At Anchorton, I was nominated to stand as CW but withdrew when a former CW decided (quite late on) to stand again – I could not see the point of contesting the election against someone who was more experienced and better qualified. The same principle of choosing candidates also applies to the election of the PCC at the APCM, and this is covered elsewhere. The only real difference is that the CWs are elected every year (and so can be challenged in any year), whereas most PCCs elect members for a set period before they need to be re-elected. This period is often three years, so that one third of the PCC members is elected each year.

The odds are that there will not be a host of volunteers to be CW; probably there won't even be any obvious candidates. Even worse, there may just be a genuine volunteer who is generally regarded as completely unsuitable. In that case, you have to take them aside and explain just what the job entails, emphasising how much work there is and the pressures of the job. However, I would also intensify the search for a well-qualified candidate, at the same time as hoping that the unsuitable volunteer will realise for himself that he won't get elected. I had a competitor once who withdrew when a respected close friend of his told him, "Yes, I think you might make a good churchwarden, but not in this church!"

What is ideally needed is a person who in some way will complement the abilities of the other CW in the unique situation of your particular church. If you are the person just elected or about to be elected, then you will have a lot to learn from the "other CW"; conversely, if the "other CW" has just been elected and you have two or three years in the job, then hopefully you will have amassed a large amount of wisdom which needs to be passed on. Identifying the responsibilities and then splitting them up between you is probably a good way to start, but even this requires hard work. It is all too easy for the CW who knows it all to carry on with everything and hardly hand over a single responsibility to the newcomer; this would not be a good move.

I would not want to pretend that I could identify the exact responsibilities of a CW in your church or indeed in any other church. This book will give you a good idea of the general responsibilities, but then the respective priorities will have to be identified locally in each individual case. Between the two of you, it is important that the responsibilities of the job are shared between both CWs (and even delegated to other PCC members, where possible) so that the burden does not fall on just one. It is also important that the one can answer in the absence of the other in times of crisis. Even if building matters are my specialist subject, I always want to make sure that my "other CW" is fully aware of the issues and things of interest, and is offered the opportunity to do interesting things, like climbing the scaffolding around the tower.

Hopefully, your vicar will want to hold regular meetings with his CWs, but you might agree to hold regular meetings for just the two of you over a coffee, especially soon after the first election of one of you. Even if you think that you already know each other well, you might well find that sharing CW responsibilities will reveal a new side of you both to each other. I have found it a real joy to watch a new CW develop in her first year or two, as she starts to understand the job, and even to enjoy it.

The Vicar

Of course, the most important member of the ministerial team for the CWs is the vicar. The CW's relationship with this person is fundamental to whether their time as CW will be of benefit to the entire parish. If the relationship is flawed, then everything that the CWs do will seem to be hard work for little reward. I know that we are meant to look towards heaven for our rewards, but we are all human, and some thanks and praise never go amiss.

There are many different types of vicar, although I did read once that the C of E has an imbalance of a particular variety. You might have heard of the Myers-Briggs Type Indicator (MBTI) which at its simplest identifies four "either-or" characteristics, giving sixteen different types of personality. I read that a particular one of these MBTI types occurred in about 18% of the general population but in 35% of Anglican priests (and they were all male at that time). Hopefully, with the introduction of women priests, that situation might have altered now, but perhaps there is something in the thought that the selection processes at the time seemed to favour people who were like the interviewers and decision-makers?

Thinking of how people become parish priests, I am convinced that one failing (to my mind) of the training is that there are many things which are omitted, such as "how to chair a PCC", "the essential laws and rules that a parish priest should know" and "how to get the best out of your flock". Those are probably my top three, but I could actually enlarge that list considerably. Closely following these is a linked couple: "how to be a training incumbent" and its converse, "how to learn and grow whilst training as a curate". Sadly, I have seen several times that the vicar-curate relationship can be unproductive and even destructive, with a curate being moved before completion of the necessary four years in post. The functioning of that relationship should be overseen by the Diocesan Director of Post-Ordination Training (or whatever your diocese wants to call that role), and it is very difficult for the CW to have any say in that relationship. Suffice it to say that if the curate takes no note of genuine constructive advice from the vicar, then he probably won't accept it from the CW either, regardless of however well-intentioned it is.

I don't often consider it my place to give the vicar some spiritual advice, but I do recall a couple of occasions while I was in the RAF. The first time, there was some discussion regarding the church fete and I vetoed the plan to have a fortune teller in a tent as they had had in previous years – 'It's only a bit of fun,' they said. The second time was when we were having a "faith lunch" and the padre could not see why I was amused when he put up a list asking for people to specify what food they were bringing to a "faith lunch". Surely if you have such a list, it's just "lunch", isn't it?

I have already mentioned that some priests are control freaks; this is most definitely NOT the way to get the best out of either the CWs or the inherited congregation! The vicar should not be authoritarian but rather a less dictatorial person who can both lead and persuade people to follow. The vicar at one parish got himself into a hole once in relation to the marriage of divorced people in church. After the PCC had discussed this, he was adamant that not only would he not marry a divorced person in church, but he would not even allow "his" church to be used for such a service by another priest (as the rules permit, but it needs the vicar's approval). He had been made aware of, but was totally unmoved by, the number of divorced people on the PCC – I think it was six; this included one woman aged fifty-odd who was married at eighteen, divorced at twenty-one, became a Christian at about twenty-five and then re-married, becoming a pillar of the church family. The entire PCC was against the vicar but he would not bend; *In Christ we are all made whole* carried no weight with him, and his entire stance was seen as being unloving to the people seated in front of him.

Another vicar seemed to delight in being hard done by, because he had to do everything himself, no one ever helped him, no one appreciated his hard work, bad things happened to him, etc. This is a most negative approach which is hard to get around – every constructive suggestion you make will be dismissed as 'We've tried that before and it didn't work' or 'That will only end up being done by me.' He once moaned at a PCC meeting about no one ever volunteering to help and then asked for someone to clear a valley gutter on the church hall roof – it was only ten feet up so was quite accessible; I said I would do it, at 9.30 on Saturday morning. I arrived promptly at 9.30 with a ladder and found that he had been up there himself for thirty minutes – a good part of the job was already done. Ask yourself if I was so quick to volunteer the next time.

On another occasion (in the RAF), I suggested organising a coach to go to hear Billy Graham in a football stadium (one of his last visits to the UK). The padre was less than enthusiastic but agreed that I could organise and advertise it, whilst at the same time saying that there would probably not be much response. I think he was quite surprised when we had thirty-six people on a forty-three seater coach one evening.

One vicar once took me aside and told me off in no uncertain terms. My "crime" was that I had sent an email to a selected group within the PCC asking if anyone had any record of a meeting with the Diocesan Advisory Committee a couple of years earlier, as I was now trying to prepare a faculty petition for some related building work; I had searched high and low without finding any such record. 'How dare you do that? Do you want people to think that we are stupid enough to come this far without that approval?' Well, it turned out that indeed we had no such approval; my email was perfectly correct and we had to get the DAC in again before we could apply for our faculty – I never received any apology.

Beware also of people who do things hastily, without thinking. Once, we were clearing the vestry before getting the builders in to do a new floor. I was fairly new and was surprised to find that the vicar's prevailing attitude was to throw things away if no one present knew of a use for any item. That might sound okay, but when there are only a few people present and no time is allowed for investigation, you are in real danger of making some wrong decisions. I did manage to retain one such item which I moved (and hid) rather than throw it away, and later found several things missing that were quite possibly thrown away then, such as key pieces of wooden tracery broken off the lectern, or the odd bit of wood broken off a choir stall – the sort of things that can be fixed easily with a bit of wood glue and some masking tape, but now sadly gone forever.

Love your vicar, and try your hardest to work with him, regardless of what other people may say. If you don't then other people will follow your lead, and so you make his job even harder.

The Ministerial Team Members

There may, of course, be many other team members. These could include a curate (who is by definition under training and is a deacon, not a priest, in the first year), some team vicars if there are the other parishes in the team, Self-Supporting Ministers (who are by definition part-time as they usually have a separate paid job), and retired clergy in the parish who have Permission to Officiate (PTO). There might also be Local Lay Ministers (who are not ordained but might be authorised to do services such as funerals). The CWs need to get on with these people; they all have their own role to play in the church, just as the CWs have their own role.

Most of them will know the role that they want to play, and the relationships might be well-defined before you become CW, so take time to get to know them.

In particular, you will find the additional priests most useful when there is an interregnum! Helping to educate the curate is perhaps one place where the CW might add value; I mentioned above some of the things that tend not be emphasised in their training, and you might find similar things yourself if you can develop that relationship. I think that if you genuinely want to help and offer occasional praise sometimes, it gives you the right to also offer constructive comments when required, whether these might be on better use of a microphone, the font size on a slide or even some aspect of liturgy. If such private comments are offered on a day when the vicar is not present, the recipient is usually pleased to be able to correct the matter when it next occurs. Of course, this also applies to the other priests, not just the curate, but then you have to be more careful with what you say if it could be seen as critical – a PTO holder might well have decades of experience as a full-time priest.

With any team member, you might be asked to contribute in a spiritual sense; frankly, this has never come easily to me and I have trouble seeing it as part of the CW job. Perhaps I ought to have done more, but I have taken my lead from the vicar and there has never been that encouragement. I have been consulted by the vicar and others on occasion – once the vicar said that she wanted to start an Alpha course and asked me to read a book about it. I read the book and was quite enthusiastic but pointed out that we didn't have the follow-on support groups available. Nevertheless, we ran the course most successfully and enjoyably with me as one of the group leaders – as I said, though, I don't see that as part of the CW job.

The PCC

The PCC are definitely part of the team with which the CWs have to work. I must confess that sometimes it has seemed to me that we might not always have been on the same team! I do feel that the conduct of a PCC meeting is quite important. I have already mentioned that I don't believe that ministers are actually trained how to chair a meeting; equally, I don't think that many PCC members have an idea of what is expected of members or how they should conduct themselves in meetings.

I recognise that I benefited from being trained in the Royal Air Force as to how to behave in meetings – arrive on time, follow the agenda, pay attention, let others speak, contribute where you add value and keep quiet if you have nothing useful to say. Accurate and brief minutes help, with actions clearly identified and allocated to specific individuals. At the next meeting, all of these actions are dealt with immediately after accepting the previous minutes, unless they are better dealt with under a specific item on the agenda. On PCCs, I have seen so many "actions" get lost by virtue of lack of clarity of minutes, but if actions are numbered then the agenda should identify each action against a specific agenda item, whether "Matters Arising" or any other item.

Over the years, I have encountered many odd views of how members see the PCC – at one church it was clear that, for many, it was the highlight of their week and so they were in no hurry to finish. Conversely, I at the time had a ninety-minute commute to and from work by train and underground, and had no real interest in an extended evening meeting; typically, after a long working day, I had precisely fifteen minutes at home to eat and change before coming out to a PCC meeting. On one occasion I arrived at the meeting straight from the train, still wearing my suit and carrying a briefcase (as one did then), but I'm not sure they noticed. Too often, there seemed to be a readiness to make jokes and exchange witty repartee even whilst I or another member was trying to inform them all of important happenings. It is still perhaps surprising that some people like to be on the PCC but never actually to take any actions as a result. One vicar used to specify that the meeting was to start at 7.15 and was actually in no hurry to start even at 7.30 due to lack of attendance, whereas my view was that we were quorate so 'Let's start please. I've had a long day.'

Now, the PCC is a legal body in its own right – it is not subservient to the diocese and the Bishop cannot actually force the PCC to do something; if the PCC votes against it, that's it. Sometimes it seems that this principle extends to minor matters arising during a meeting, and on a few occasions I have felt that the members and I were on opposite sides. What I have found is that if you then raise the same thing at a later meeting, you might well get agreement that time. Once, my powers of persuasion failed me, and it seemed that they just wanted to vote against my proposal for no reason other than spite. They then approved it at the next meeting without argument!

PCC meetings are one of the times when I am convinced that most members have no idea of the amount of work done by a CW between meetings. The lack of attention and understanding at times has been astonishing and, frankly, a bit disappointing. To me it shows that they do not really care about what the CW does, or the amount of work required for the CW to be able to report back to the PCC. They are happy to pass the buck to the CW but appear to have no interest in what the CW actually has done on their behalf. People might say that they appreciate the work that you do, but that doesn't mean much if they don't really understand the full extent of your efforts.

The Church Administrator

If you are fortunate, you will have some sort of administrator in the team or parish. If you are really fortunate, this person will be reliable, conscientious, a wizard with computers and able to do three hours' work in a single hour. Such a person is absolutely indispensible and should be loved and cared for because her departure would be sorely felt by you and the whole team. Make sure that she gets paid a sensible amount and check that the PCC has sorted out their responsibilities for workplace pensions.

I would point out that the odds are that this person is not the vicar's own personal assistant but is employed for the benefit of the entire team. The CW needs to know who the line manager is and who pays for the administrator. It is the line manager's job to make sure that the administrator is not over-tasked by team members but, equally, the line manager must not personally fill the administrator's time to the exclusion of all others! A fair balance must be found.

The Church Organist

It might seem odd that I single out the church organist as another important member of the team, but I think that good ones are hard to come by; if you have a good one then be sure to keep her. Just wait until she has an unexpected crisis, a long holiday, or else decides to move church. You will then have to find some stand-in and will realise just how good and reliable she was.

We do tend to have a regular stand-in for most funerals but on occasion have had to find someone from afar. I have had to introduce one such organist to our organ, and my own knowledge stretched as far as unlocking it and switching it on. The thing that a visitor must not do is to change the settings for the stops – this is guaranteed to annoy the regular organist.

I know of one organist whose favourite mischief in the service is to play appropriately titled pieces of music when the opportunity presents itself, such as Handel's *Water Music* during the ablutions, or the *Star Wars March* during a procession. Of course, you have to recognise it enough to know the title, so it's usually only a few (such as the choir) who get the joke.

The Church Cleaner

It is so easy to take the cleaner for granted, especially if she is a paid person, but that is no justification. There should be a clear specification of what she should clean and, importantly, what she should NOT clean. For instance, you might not want her to clean any ancient leaded windows, or use nasty modern cleaning materials on mediaeval floor tiles. Also, don't forget that someone has to buy these cleaning materials.

6

Church Services

The major visible part of the CW's job is attending church services. The amount of services (or other events) where attendance is required is very much a local question, according to how the CW is used, the other staff available and the number of people at each service. The requirement may change accordingly for the more unusual services where large numbers of the public are expected, such as large funerals or Remembrance.

At Clamcester, we have three services every Sunday morning, and attendance by a CW at each was mandated by a previous vicar. Consequently, some Assistant CWs (ACWs) were appointed to share some of the burden (see *Rotas*). In fact, the last of the three services on a Sunday morning used to have two CWs in attendance, but in the interregnum I made the decision that, with numbers slightly falling, there really was no need for this duplication and so now there is only one; even that is hard to fill sometimes.

Regular Services

In many ways, as I mentioned earlier, you could regard the CW role in church services as a combination of the jobs of stage manager and front of house manager in a theatre. In my view, the CW has to make sure that everything happens at the right time and in the right way, apart from what the principals actually say and do in front of the congregation. You might think that everything is straightforward and routine – the same people do the same thing every week, after all – so what could possibly go wrong?

The answer is "lots"! As we use more technology in services, there is an increasing scope for new ways of things going wrong, but even with the "old way", people still seem to be able to devise new and ingenious ways of making something go wrong. A CW can never really relax and think it is all under control because that is bound to be the moment that the fire alarm decides to activate, or the sidesperson has a complete brain fade and does something silly, or the vestry table collapses noisily with no one near it. I will admit that the technology has a lot to answer for, although strictly it would probably be more accurate to say "the operator of the technology". Mind you, once, the slides went haywire and it wasn't the operator's fault – we had a new pointer and for the first time the preacher had operated them from the front. He then put the pointer in his pocket, and every time he moved, he wasn't aware that it was still operating the slides. I was really puzzled for a few minutes…

The CW's job is to anticipate every possible requirement of the service, taking into account the personnel involved and the complexity of the service, and to do everything he can to resolve potential issues before they cause major disruption. In fact, I would say that this is probably the major downside of the job as far as I am concerned – you are constantly on call, on alert or in demand, and it is very hard to actually participate in the worship. That might be just me, but somehow I think many CWs would share in that sentiment.

Let's think of a few of the things that I check before a service:

1. Is there someone doing the AV? Is he competent or do I need to sit close to him?
2. Has anything been changed at the last minute in the AV presentation? Or is there a film clip to be shown? (Both of these are always a source of danger.)
3. Are the microphones out and switched on? (Once, as the choir were processing in, I saw from five pews back that the battery light on the lectern microphone was red, and so hurriedly got a replacement microphone. I left the old one on and kept it beside me – it died during the Gospel reading.)
4. Is the camera working today? (Ours is a bit temperamental and sometimes sulks.)
5. Are the screens displaying correctly? (I think ours are upset by incorrectly large margins on pictures.)
6. Are there any banns to be read? (The vicar might have already tucked the book somewhere, but do check – you might find yourself running to the vestry during the service to get it. In the absence of an ordained minister, the job of reading them falls to the CW – and it is a real pleasure!)
7. Do I have two sidespeople?
8. Do I have a Lay Eucharistic Assistant for the chalice (if a Eucharist)?

9. Is there someone to read the Bible? (At Bogthornly, I probably used to read about once per month due to the failure of the person on the rota to turn up. Having not noticed beforehand, I would find the reading as I walked down to the front, hoping it had no difficult words in it.)

10. Is someone doing the coffee? Have they remembered to bring some milk?

11. Is there anyone new in church (especially a banns couple)? Has someone greeted them, or do I have time to do that?

12. Is there a couple who have agreed to take the elements up at the offertory?

13. Is there anything odd or unusual planned? If so, check what is required with whoever is planning it.

14. Finally, do I have that nagging feeling of having missed something? This includes things that other people do, like lighting the candles. I have learned to check everything again if I get that feeling, and I often find (as age increases) that I have indeed forgotten something.

Occasional Offices

This is a grand term for baptisms, marriages and funerals (also referred to as "hatch, match and despatch"). We don't supply a CW for these, but for weddings and funerals we expect there to be a paid verger who is often one of the CWs or ACWs. The verger is the minister's help in everything, as there is likely to be no other church member at those services other than the organist (so if there is a visiting minister and a visiting organist, it's all down to the verger). As a result, the verger needs to be able to be in tune with the minister, controlling the microphones, CD player and lights if needed, as well as opening the doors. The aim is to be "professional" if one can use that word: we want those attending to go home with a positive memory of the church or, at least, no negative memories of errors caused by the AV, for instance.

For funerals, families these days will often select some music to be played at the entrance and the recessional. The choice of music can be pretty poor at times and, hopefully, this will have been improved by pre-funeral visiting by the minister. *Bat out of Hell* is one suggestion that sounds pretty inappropriate! Once, there was a rap for the recessional which was said to have some unacceptable words on it, but when we checked beforehand we could hardly understand a single word, so we played it anyway. I also recall one funeral for a dear lady who was a stalwart of our congregation, although her family did not share her faith. When her coffin was carried out, the family had chosen *My Way* as the music – I cannot think of a less appropriate song for such a woman of faith.

A major pitfall at a funeral is when there are tributes to be read by family members; it is essential to try to find out beforehand who these people are and brief them on their relationship with the microphone – they tend to assume that if they are standing near the microphone then it can pick them up. If a child is to speak, supply a second microphone on a stand at a different height so that she can be heard as well; it does nothing for anyone if such a tribute is inaudible. If all else fails, brief the minister to be ready to move the microphone if/when needed so that all the tributes can be heard, including that of the tearful little granddaughter!

The other funeral pitfall is the hymns. The choice of hymns these days is often quite limited, and you can guarantee that even with a congregation of fifty or one hundred, the singing is going to be pretty poor; if you have fewer than fifty then probably you and the minister will be singing a duet. It does baffle me how a family can choose apparently well-known hymns and yet still fail to sing them; at my funeral I want three or four good Christian hymns of praise and worship which all my family and friends will sing loudly and properly. Nowadays, the standard ones seem to be *All things bright and beautiful, Abide with me, The Lord's my Shepherd, The day Thou gavest Lord is ended, The Old Rugged Cross* and *Jerusalem.* Without a doubt, the worst of these for a congregation to sing is *Jerusalem.* This is because, if they are not familiar with it, they have no idea of when to start singing either verse. I once heard of a complaint about the organist after a funeral. It so happened I had been the verger at that service and I knew that the congregation had had no idea of how to sing *Jerusalem*, yet they thought the problem was the organist's bad playing.

For baptisms, we have a team who visit the family beforehand, and the same person does the verger/CW role at the service as well. In most cases, the family are not familiar with the church, and this provides a friendly and known face to welcome them.

Unusual Services

These are essentially the civic events (at Clamcester, we have a civic service each year, as well as Remembrance), plus things like school carol services or the Scout service where they just want someone to let them in, and perhaps some help with microphones and lights.

Remembrance is a pretty big deal at Clamcester. For the 11am two minutes' silence and wreath-laying, we will usually have about 800 people around the war memorial outside the church, and about 600 of these then cram into the church for the main service. This is where your organisation and delegation skills come to the fore, as there is no way that two CWs can be everywhere at the same time. Seating that number of people in a matter of four or five minutes is a feat in itself, but every year we manage to produce the goods. The thing that really puzzles me is that the town council seem to think that we start every time with a clean sheet of paper, rather than starting with last year's programme and just sorting what went wrong. We and the Royal British Legion have a pretty good idea of how to do it by now!

The point about the occasional and unusual services is that they will bring into the church many people who do not often attend, yet they still have some sort of expectation about the event. It might well be a pretty negative expectation, in which case I as CW really want to ensure that nothing affirms that expectation. At the very least, I want to ensure that the service itself goes without a hitch, and I want to do my bit towards making them feel welcome. Ideally, it is nice to confound their negative expectations, such as when a parent goes to take a child outside and I can direct them to the (fairly new) toilet, which even has a changing mat for babies! Going back to the theatre metaphor, I want everyone, especially the visitors, to enjoy the "performance".

I like lists, so here's another one. These are some of the odd things that have happened in a church service, which illustrate the sort of thing a CW has to be on guard for during a service:

1. Youths outside throwing a stone, which broke a leaded window.
2. Someone at the back loudly asking the preacher a question during his sermon at the midnight Eucharist on Christmas Eve.
3. Drunks who come in at the midnight Eucharist on Christmas Eve (I always ask a couple of large male friends to be ready in case anything nasty happens, but it never has).
4. The fire alarm going off (do other people know how to turn it off?).
5. Someone bringing his dog into the church. I tolerated it whilst he was talking quietly near the door and ignoring the service, but when he started to walk the dog over to the far side of the church where the coffee was being prepared, I decided enough was enough and asked him to stay beside the door.
6. The person on the reading rota staying seated when it is time for the first lesson (never assume – check that they know it is their turn).
7. A display of flowers in full view at the very front of the nave deciding to fall over (due to imbalance as the water evaporated) – and that was at a major service at Christmas.
8. The microphones not working at all – once, I forgot to bring the wireless controller out. Another time, someone had switched the system off and on again, which disconnected said wireless controller even though the light remained on as usual.

9. Horrible feedback on the microphones – usually caused by poor positioning of the throat microphone or by the minister standing in exactly the bad spot that we all know about.

10. The organ dying during Widor's *Toccata* at a wedding – this happened at Bogthornly, where the pump for the organ was simply not big enough if too much air was demanded of it. I did warn the organist about it at the rehearsal, but he ignored me and then discovered for himself that it really does sound dreadful when an organ dies of asphyxiation.

11. The music group playing so loudly before the service that you cannot conduct a conversation at the far end of the church.

12. Discovering the hard way at Remembrance that one of the Brownie pennants on a tubular metal pole does not hold together very well – it really clangs when the end drops off onto the tiled floor.

13. Realising at the same Remembrance service that there had to be a way of ensuring that each standard-bearer received the right item at the end of the service, but I didn't know what it was.

14. Candles at the Carols by Candlelight service dripping wax onto a lady wearing a nice coat.

15. The Advent wreath catching fire at the start of the service on Epiphany because the candles had burned down among the greenery, but the verger had lit them anyway.

16. The Paschal Candle refusing to light from the fire outside at the Easter Dawn service due to the very high wind.

17. Being disturbed by a council road sweeper who pushed his barrow noisily across the churchyard at 6am on Easter Sunday during another Dawn service.

18. Realising that the vicar was touching his laptop at intervals, but the screen was not changing to his next slide – how do you tell him after half the sermon?
19. Hearing the sound of someone on the church roof at night, when they had evaded the alarmed scaffolding erected round the tower.
20. People who want to organise a meeting with you or ask you to pass a message to your wife, but ask this during the Peace.

I want to add something here about worship and music in services. A well-played organ and a good worship leader are both great – I know that some will love one and despise the other, but I am sure that there is room in our churches for both. However, there is one thing that really gets me and it is when a worship leader, usually with a guitar, starts performing as opposed to leading worship. For me, there is a clear distinction here; I must stress that this is nothing to do with any of the churches where I have worshipped regularly, but rather I have experienced it at a couple of Christian festivals.

At one of these festivals, a well-known young woman led the morning worship brilliantly – she led the congregation of 2,000 in worship of God. In the evening, it was the turn of the other so-called worship leader who clearly did not realise how far he had strayed from his brief. He performed with his band as though it was some music concert which happened to include Christian songs; at one stage, he was jamming with one of his guitarists and certainly enjoying himself, but you had to be a mind reader to know where we were in the song and what we were meant to sing next. In fact, there were long bits where we weren't meant to sing at all but rather just admire their undoubted skill. This was totally performance and not worship – certainly it did nothing for me and a large part of the congregation; admittedly there were some who were enjoying themselves, but I can't believe that even they thought that was worship, surely?

I mentioned the banns book earlier. If there is no priest or deacon at the service then under the Marriage Act 1949 the duty of reading the banns may be done by a lay person. I actually like doing this, especially if one of the couples is in church and I have managed to speak to them before the service. I would always do this myself rather than let an assistant CW do it, but if there is a priest present then they should always get to do it, even if they are not leading the service. We try to read the banns at the end of the service rather than the beginning as quite often a couple would turn up late and so miss hearing their own banns!

The reading of banns is one thing that I have made sure is done properly; it puzzled me that priests would often say, "If anyone knows any reason why they should not marry, you are to declare it now", and then add, "Silence is good" or some other silly comment. The word "now" is not on the helpful bookmark which is kept in our banns book, and so I never said that. Then I realised – the officiant has to say "Now" when this line is said in the marriage ceremony because it's the last chance, but it is not to be said when banns are called.

As a matter of fact, I don't believe that my own banns were correctly read. The Marriage Act 1949 Section 12(2) says that the marriage must then take place within three months of the completion of reading banns. We received a banns certificate from the parish of my wife's parents giving three dates in March even though we were getting married in the middle of July. We pointed out that this was not correct and duly received another certificate giving dates in April; however, my mother-in-law-to-be said that she was there on at least one of those days and never heard our names. I have been assured that incorrect reading of banns does not give grounds for annulment!

7

The Archdeacon's
Inspection

To share responsibilities between the CWs, you first
need to identify what actually needs to be done. A good
place to start is the Archdeacon's Annual Inspection
(sometimes referred to as a Visitation, but this confuses
with other "Visitations" such as the churchwardens'
swearing-in). Prior to the inspection, you should be
asked to complete the "Articles of Enquiry" which is
a formal set of questions, usually the same each year,
sometimes with "this year's special question" tacked
on the end. For some reason, the special question is
not usually advertised in advance, although I think in
some cases it would make life easier if they told you at
the start of the year. However, there is much more to
be checked than just the Articles of Enquiry, and there
should normally be a checklist provided of what will be
checked on this occasion. In essence, this checklist is the
basis of the practical list of tasks for the CWs; if you can
answer all the questions well, then you must be doing a
good part of the job.

Hopefully, these annual inspections are done in your diocese. I believe that they are rightly done by the Archdeacon, but he may delegate some or all of them to the Area/Rural Deans. At Bogthornly, the Archdeacon did one third of them each year, which meant that every three years he personally inspected every church in his charge – that Archdeacon is now a diocesan bishop. Sadly, not every diocese is so conscientious, and the diocese at Clamcester actually only reinstated these inspections three years ago after a very long absence, then a year later they didn't happen as "we were all too busy"!

For me, this inspection is very important. The point of it is largely just to make the CWs do all these routine things – if the inspection is not done, then a church can "get away with it" for years, as there is no other way of the diocese finding out how bad things are. I am a firm believer in the principle of getting the basics right to give the church a stable foundation; if you don't, then one or more of these will bite you in the future, usually at the very worst moment. My view is that these inspections are essential as they then push the CWs into some sort of attempt at doing the necessary work. Failure to do them encourages an individual approach which allows people to do what they want and ignore the rest. I am afraid to say that most of my predecessors as CW in two parishes had very little idea of these fundamentals of the job; one, who was CW for nine years, said he had never heard of the Archdeacon's (or Area Dean's) inspections.

The checklist for the inspection should include roughly the same standard items for all churches (which are covered in detail on the pages following):

1. Date of last inspections and checks:
   - Fire extinguishers
   - Fire alarm system
   - Electrical system
   - Portable Appliance Testing
   - Gas boiler
   - Lightning conductor
2. Inventory
3. Log book
4. Recent faculties
5. Date of the last Quinquennial Inspection (QI)
6. Outstanding issues from Quinquennial Inspection Report (QIR)
7. Service registers
8. PCC minutes
9. APCM minutes
10. Annual report (includes finances)
11. Annual parish returns
12. Insurance cover and certificates displayed?
13. Health and Safety
14. Accident book and first aid kit available and up to date?
15. Safeguarding
16. Disability provision
17. Asbestos

You get the picture! This is not the full job, just some fundamentals; but even so it's a pretty long list, and the trick is to be virtually up to date with all these as a matter of course, even if the inspection is not done every year; then when the inspection comes, all you are really doing is checking them, not doing them all at the last minute.

One item on this list slightly annoys me. There is no legal requirement that I can find for the CWs being responsible for the state of the registers (although this is mentioned in the *Guide to the Duties of a CW* mentioned earlier). Nevertheless, they will be checked at this inspection and it then looks bad if you try to evade the responsibility. It is much easier if you do accept this responsibility and frequently keep an eye on these, although one cannot help but think that CWs have enough to do in any case!

I have been surprised at a number of errors or omissions that often occur in registers:

- You should use the correct archival quality pen, as most modern ballpoints will fade surprisingly quickly; I once found the Bishop using his own, rather than the correct one resting on the register.
- Many ministers forget to sign at all, and so I enter the initials in pencil and get them to sign later, sometimes even months later! Clutching the unsigned register, I have twice had to run after the same Bishop to the car park.
- At Anchorton and Bogthornly, I was accustomed to the priest at a Eucharist counting wafers and so being able to enter the number of communicants, but then at Clamcester, I often found that neither the priest nor the server had any idea of the number. I remain convinced that both of them are better placed (literally) than the CW to do this.
- Even if I am not the duty CW, I tend to count the congregation automatically – it is often forgotten and people's estimates after the event can be wildly wrong, so it helps if you have a good idea.
- A new service register had the columns for adults and children in the opposite order to the old one (why do they change these things?), and people persisted in entering these figures wrongly for ages.

- The burial register was being used incorrectly, to record interments where the body was buried in the town council's cemetery. Our churchyard was closed for burials as long ago as 1855, and the only records that should be made are for the interment of ashes, which is allowed by faculty. (A funeral service itself is of course recorded in the service register.)

- Completed baptism and wedding registers should be sent to the Local Records Office (or equivalent), not kept by the parish, except possibly for the last completed one which may often be referred to. I think this change came in at some time in the mid 20th century when it was realised that some churches did not look after these legal documents well, if at all, and many had been lost by fire or dampness. In my view, a Records Office has professionals whose job it is to look after documents such as these, so use them.

The Quinquennial Inspection is a detailed check of the church building, performed by the church architect. The resulting Quinquennial Inspection Report (QIR) is the second starting point for what CWs need to do, as it contains recommendations for items of work, some of which should be done immediately and some others urgently. The CWs need to be very familiar with the recommendations of the QIR and have an action plan to act on them; the Archdeacon or Area Dean will expect some familiarity with the recommendations.

There is a complete chapter on the QI and QIR later on when I move on to the subject of looking after the church building, but it is such a fundamental item that it deserves mention here as well. If the architect does not remind you that this inspection is due, then you should remind him in plenty of time.

The rest of the inspection list above is pretty standard, and much of it is covered in detail in the chapter on Fundamental Tasks. If you have kept up to date with all these things, it is the work of only a few minutes to muster an impressively large pile of registers, ring binders and other files for the inspection. When the Area Dean did our most recent inspection (her first here), she reported that it was a "model inspection", which made me quite smug; but it isn't really that difficult. Of course, if you are not up to date then there will be quite a bit of work to do before the inspection, so prepare well in advance.

In my opinion, this inspection is a matter for just the CWs; the vicar does not need to be present – indeed, you may actually not want her to be there. In the Archdeacon's list in one diocese, the last question was "Is there anything you would like to tell me or ask me that hasn't been covered?" Now, if you wish to make any comment about the vicar or curate, this is your chance. At one of these inspections, I said, "Yes, there is", and the Archdeacon replied, "I thought there would be!" To raise something difficult about a priest is much easier in this sort of situation than having to ask for an appointment and go to meet the Archdeacon at the diocese; if you have an issue such as a difficult vicar-CW relationship, or a difficult vicar-curate relationship or even the vicar generally losing his way (and congregation), then if you haven't already raised it, now is the time. Even if the matter is just a "concern" as opposed to an actual "issue", I would recommend raising it at this inspection rather than keeping it bottled up. On the other hand, if it's really bad then you definitely should have raised it already – don't think you have to wait for the inspection.

8

Fundamental Tasks

Church Inventory

The church inventory is a very useful document – well, it certainly will be the day that the church is gutted by fire or you suffer a burglary; you will then want to prove to the insurers exactly what possessions the church has lost (and hence possibly their value). Just don't keep the only copy of the inventory in the church as well!

The inventory should be revised annually to make sure that it is up to date, and signed accordingly, usually at the time of the Archdeacon's Inspection. You also need to tell the APCM each year that you have checked it and that everything is present and correct – this is, sadly, easy to gloss over and treat lightly ('no one else will know...').

The inventory is actually quite tedious to produce the first time but, once it's done, it all becomes pretty easy to maintain if you do it properly. You can buy the special ring binder and pages for the inventory from Church House. I found at Bogthornly that the only inventory was a three-page list covered with handwritten amendments by the vicar, so I decided to revise it completely and produced my own soft copy on my PC in exactly the same format as the official one (other than the page numbers). I don't recommend permanent handwritten changes, but they can be used during the year until the inventory is brought up to date in preparation for the Inspection, when new pages can be printed as required. I put a date on each page and, when amended and reprinted, the old page was filed at the back of the inventory so that a record of all changes was available.

At Clamcester, I found that the inventory had last been revised twenty-one years previously (and then eighteen more years before that, in pencil!), so I found my old template and used that again to produce an up-to-date inventory from scratch. This inventory was eventually inspected by the Area Dean doing the Archdeacon's Inspection, when I said that surely it was about time that the diocese got up to date and issued it as a soft copy for everyone. To my surprise, six months later, this actually happened!

The inventory has to describe every item in sufficient detail (material, size, inscriptions, etc.), accompanied by a photograph (or even a set of photographs) of each item. You need to devise a numbering system so that the same number defines the item in the inventory and can also be written on small adhesive labels on the relevant photograph. The actual photographs do not need to be works of art, just enough to sufficiently identify each item, so that might need more than one photograph of some items. Put a ruler beside items such as silver to give a good indication of size, and also take a photo of the hallmark. A soft copy of the photographs should be kept with the soft copy of the inventory in more than one place where they will not be lost, but a hard copy set should be kept with the printed inventory. I bought one of those small airtight sandwich boxes of a suitable size, which has proved ideal.

At Clamcester, when we had some painted glass windows vandalised, the only good thing was the gratification that I was able to produce a recent digital photograph of the windows as they existed before the damage. Had I not done the inventory, I doubt that such a good photo would have existed.

Church Silver

Most churches will possess some items of silver – normally those used during the Eucharist – and all silver must be detailed on the church inventory. Some churches will possess a lot more silver, possibly mediaeval and intricate, historic and precious; most people would think that a church is especially blessed to possess such silver. Actually, the reverse is true. To the CWs, it has no value; rather, it is actually a liability, as it has to be cared for and insured. Silver items of significant value cannot safely be kept in a church nowadays without significant expenditure on security, and if you display them as many people would like, then the risks and costs are even greater.

Worse, in many cases you cannot sell them either. You might want to sell them to fund a building programme, but you need permission in the form of a faculty to sell the silver. However, the general principle is that you can only sell such items if there is a clear need for the benefit of the church which can only be met by such a sale; even then, if the items have a local connection, you have virtually no chance of being granted that faculty. You might also find that they are not worth as much as you might think. At Bogthornly, the previous vicar and her CWs had found this out the hard way: the major items had been valued many years previously, and someone had increased this with inflation to arrive at a vast overestimate of their actual market value; however, it was found that the potential net income would be barely £10,000 rather than the anticipated £80,000-£100,000. Moreover, of the nine major items, seven have local inscriptions (one has a link to William Shakespeare!) and so in all probability they will never be allowed to sell those.

Just because items are unsellable does not mean that they are worthless, of course, although they do have a zero value in the church accounts until you have a faculty to sell them. These items still need to be properly secured and insured so they can actually cost the church money every year. Most banks have now ceased their free storage for such items, so you either need to pay for this facility or else spend money on physical security in the church.

There is one alternative if any of your silver is of genuine importance: you might then be able to have it looked after by someone such as the cathedral museum (if there is one) or even by a major museum such as the Victoria and Albert Museum, who would then be responsible for the security. Such loans are normally for a few years only, but they should write to you asking if you would extend the loan. In such a case, all you have to do is make sure that it is recorded as such in the inventory.

Church Log Book

The church log book is another of those CW-type mysteries that most people tend to ignore even if they do happen to hear about it. The log book is a record of all the things that happen to the church building over each quinquennium (a defined five-year period), and you can buy the hard copy pages for a twenty-five-year period from Church House, to fit in a ring binder. The idea is that this book forms a permanent record of everything that has been done to the church building in that twenty-five-year period, so obviously the old log books should be kept as well.

However, I have to say that I have never seen a log book which had been kept for more than ten years previously. I am afraid that most of my predecessors had no idea of what should be included, and I admit it did take me a while to get a feel for what was required.

Each five-year period starts with a Quinquennial Inspection (QI), and so the main thing to include is a copy of the QI Report (QIR). You then also file in it the following:

1. Every routine check or inspection, such as the current Certificates of Inspection for the following:
    - Gas boiler
    - Portable Appliance Testing
    - Lightning conductor testing
    - Fire alarm inspection
    - Electrical system check
2. Every faculty with detailed plans (or where to find those details)
3. Details of all work done which was required by the QIR

4. Details of any other major work not requiring a faculty (if there is such a category!)
5. Current insurance certificate(s)

You only need to keep in the log book the current certificates for (1) and (5) above – I suggest you remove the old ones for (1) and either file or recycle them. The old insurance certificates, however, must be filed carefully forever as they are proof that you were insured at a particular time, which is just a bit useful when a former employee sues you for something that happened ten or twenty years ago. Also, don't get rid of the legal embossed copy of faculty certificates.

You do not need to include minor maintenance work in the log book, but I always keep a list of that as well, as it impresses the Archdeacon. In fact, a decent maintenance plan is a useful reminder of what needs doing, when it was last done and when it needs doing again.

Rotas

It is, I am sure, a fact that no one likes producing church rotas; at least, after all these years, I am sure that I have never heard anyone admit it. In fact, it is pretty rare for anyone to even offer praise for the poor soul who picked up this job by not paying full attention at a PCC meeting. However, a church runs on doing largely routine things, and a rota is the best (only?) way of controlling not only the minister for each service but also the volunteers who do the myriad tasks required each Sunday (as well as other days).

Gone are the days of the same vicar taking a single service in the same church every Sunday, with the same organist, same verger and same sidesman each week. Many vicars these days have more than one church and are likely to be the first person out after a service as they rush off to their next service at a different church, where there waits a set of volunteers nervously checking their watches as the hour approaches. Gone also are the days when it was a rare honour to read the lesson – you actually rehearsed carefully in church before standing nervously at the polished brass lectern with the Bible on the eagle's wings, and over a hundred pairs of eyes on you.

The issue these days seems to be finding enough willing volunteers (there's that word again) to fill all the gaps. Admittedly, we now have more jobs for people to do, as there were no AV operators in those days, and coffee after a service was pretty rare, but it seems that in these modern times we have lost some of the sense of routine duty. I think some of this change has come about because of a desire to involve more people in each service, but possibly those involved actually decided that they would like a few Sundays off a particular duty.

At Clamcester, we normally have three services on a Sunday morning, and it was decided a long time ago that there should be a CW at every service. Therefore, a small number of Assistant Churchwardens (ACWs) were appointed to ease the burden on the two CWs (a good example of how you can delegate to make your CW job easier). With two sidespeople at each of the two main services, chalice assistants, an AV operator and with a server and crucifer at one of these, we end up with needing to fill something like sixteen rota slots on any one Sunday, not counting the ministers and lay leadership team who are on a separate rota and might have between five and eight slots to fill, according to the particular Sunday.

I think we would all say that we lead busy lives nowadays, partly I guess because travel is so easy – we can go to visit family or friends, we can go on holiday, we can visit another church, we might have to work on Sunday, and some might be working away from home for a week or two, possibly even abroad. The demands of modern life, especially those with a young family and those couples who both work, all add up a great proportion of the congregation being unable to commit themselves to a particular day. When they can get to church as a family, the last thing they want to do is to split the family whilst one does some useful job. It all makes it immensely difficult to fill the rota, and I have found that it often falls to the CW to find someone at short notice – hence the appointment of ACWs to share the load.

I would like to suggest some way of finding volunteers and of making them do as they promised, but I don't know anything that works reliably. It's certainly pretty irritating when the promised person fails to turn up and the overworked CW has to step into the breach yet again.

Many times at Bogthornly, I found that the nominated reader was not there at the due time; it was impossible to check with any certainty before the service as so many people arrived late! The simple answer each time then was to do it myself. I was most disappointed one Sunday when the reader arrived just in time to read, as I had seen that it was Matthew's gospel and the call of Matthew, which I was looking forward to reading as, curiously, I have never read that passage in church.

I recall one church in the RAF where our ever-present organist would only do the reading on just a particular Sunday each year – I forget the passage or why this was important to him. One Sunday, I realised that it was his turn and saw him at the organ, so never gave a thought to check with him before the service. The time for the reading came, and he sat still. I stood up, picked up a Bible, turned to the page as I walked down the aisle and read the lesson, sight unseen. Afterwards, he said to me, 'I should have been reading that – I didn't realise until you were on the fourth verse!' Thereafter, I have always checked with each individual that they are ready to do the duty which I am expecting them to do – it is not enough to know simply that they are present on the right day.

Filing

Filing is a pretty boring subject. No one can ever really see the need for it, and it tends to be regarded as unnecessary retrospection when we should be looking to the future. I have found two methods of filing in use: either everything is in one huge pile in the vicar's office (to which you do not have access), or it is held in the homes of the previous officers (CWs, treasurer, secretary) of the church, probably unsorted in a set of carrier bags. This sort of thing is really unhelpful, as you will quickly find when you are asked about anything that took place before your election.

So, I believe that a decent filing system is needed. You need to give this some thought, according to what is happening in your church, but there are some fundamentals which apply to everyone. Of course, nowadays, files are in both hard and soft copy; I would not advocate that you need to print off every single email that you receive, but there are some emails which you know need to be kept for a good while, so do print off the selected important ones. A lot of these are financial or relating to the building: specialist reports (asbestos, bats, archaeology, etc.), invoices (never pay an invoice without writing on the hard copy), end-of-year accounts, DAC visit reports, comments from relevant organisations about faculty petitions and so on. These are the things that one day you (or your successor) will be searching for with growing frustration, and a search for a hard copy report is so much easier than looking for a soft copy on any one of a number of laptops and memory sticks.

There are some ways of not doing filing. I knew one person in the RAF who filed every piece of correspondence meticulously, in a large envelope for each month. The trouble was that he never actually seemed to do more than read these once; he certainly never actioned any request for his input. Don't be like that. I never file anything away until I have actioned it, as filing is one way of losing actions which need to be done. Hence I suggest using personal files for actions relating to the PCC and the church building, but make sure that you have copies and that the masters are correctly filed. These personal files contain only the latest things which are still current and, by only having a couple of such files, I am less likely to lose anything. Note that I do not say that I don't lose anything – you have to accept that as part of the package as you get older!

At Bogthornly, the vicar was, as I have said earlier, a real control freak. He hardly delegated anything to his CWs or anyone else, and hence was always complaining about the amount of work he had to do. The trouble was that he had no filing system, just large piles of stuff on his desk (in the vicarage) where no one else could ever see it. This nearly caused us a major expense once:

The trouble started when a member of a different church (who hired our building) got an electric shock from their musical items stored under our stairs, even though the mains input and meter was elsewhere. When I checked, it was apparent that, when the meter had been moved out of there some years previously, a bare brass terminal had been left live. We got the problem fixed quickly by the supplier and then, some two months later, we received a bill for about £2,000, citing our "illegal work under the church floor".

The vicar was in favour of getting the other church to pay this, but I managed to take the bill from him and said that I would deal with it. Within a few hours, I had written a very forceful and succinct letter to the supplier, copied to our insurer, explaining the situation and stating why we would not be paying their outrageous bill; I concluded by saying that they should be very relieved that our church had not burned down as a result of their negligence in doing the original work, which would have caused our insurers to pursue them for £6 million! They politely caved in and withdrew the bill, and I thought no more of it.

However, there was a sequel: when we employed an administrator a couple of years later, she went through the piles from the vicar's desk and filed everything in some nice new files. A while later, I looked at the "Electricity" file for something and found, to my astonishment, a letter from the supplier which predated the £2,000 bill. In this they asked us to tell them why we should not pay for that emergency work or else they would issue a bill within four weeks if we didn't answer! Do you see what I mean about the need for a filing system and not losing items that need action?

Day of Rest

Most clergy make sure that they have a day of rest each week – well, the ones in my experience do as they realise that the way to a breakdown is to work continually. For them, it really is essential to have a day that they can call their own, when they are not available for meetings or to answer the phone or do a funeral or even to check their emails. All CWs should also observe this and not disturb them if at all possible, and also encourage other people to do likewise.

In the same way, as CW, you need to try to have a day which is your own. If you are at all busy and involved as CW, you will find that life does start to get on top of you sometimes. People will always do things at times of their own convenience: they will arrange meetings, organise deliveries, expect immediate answers to emails and treat you as the first person to ask when there is a visitor who wants to be shown around church. It will always be the case that members of the congregation will not understand how much time the CWs devote to their job, even if they are doing it only partly properly. The only possible exceptions are previous CWs who do usually understand, but even then their view of the job may have been a lot different to your own.

In my term as CW at Bogthornly, I was living two miles from the church and working full-time. Hence people's expectations of me then were slightly less demanding, and so the day of rest was not really an issue for me. I was also helped by the fact that my wife was doing a PhD part-time, so most Saturdays I went to the church and could do some quite major jobs, just to get out of her way. Now I am retired (from paid employment, at least) and live opposite the church at Clarncester; I knew when we bought this house that there would be a commitment as convenient key-holder even if I didn't ever become CW.

It was during our interregnum that the idea of a CW's day of rest was suggested to me – I had never really thought of it before. I tried hard in those fourteen months to put it into practice, but it just never worked as we CWs were just too busy as we were presented with the sort of thing that the vicar copes with on a daily basis. However, things settled down with the new vicar and a year later I started to volunteer with the local wildlife trust; the working party met every Tuesday, which happened also to be the day when I go square dancing in the evening. Although this made for a tiring Tuesday, it got me out of the house and away from the church, and slowly people started to get the idea that Tuesdays were bad for me. Neither of these events was essential, and I did make exceptions when Tuesday was the only day that the vicar could make, but the principle was set.

Recently, I have stopped the wildlife volunteering as it was exacerbating my bad back, but most people haven't realised that I have stopped. So Tuesdays now are more of a genuine day of rest, when I can choose what I want to do without distraction and interference. So I thoroughly recommend that CWs should try to have a day of rest each week, just as clergy should.

I mentioned square dancing above. I started to learn this at the end of the interregnum, even though I'm not in any way a dancing sort of person. Although I can demonstrate physical coordination in all sorts of sports and other activities, I have never managed to dance – the coordination of hands and feet to a rhythm always seems to elude me and I feel silly (and I think I probably look silly as well!). However, I reckon that square dancing appeals to me as it's not that sort of dancing. Rather than following a set sequence of moves, the caller calls out each move from a large number of options and you have to concentrate very hard to execute it; what matters is getting your body in the right place at the right time, preferably facing the right way, and it doesn't matter as a beginner whether you took four or seven steps to get there. In fact, in a square of two beginners with little knowledge and six fairly good dancers, the beginners can be gently pushed or otherwise guided around by the six and so achieve a pretty good end result which is most satisfying. So, rather to my surprise, I have got on well in four years and have found it to be a very good source of exercise for both body and mind.

Come to think of it, to have someone calling out your next move does have a certain analogy to the life of a CW – you never know what is coming next, and it is easy to be a step behind if you don't pay attention. Moreover, sometimes we go round in circles, which also sounds a bit familiar. However, if you and your team can work together then the result creates a good deal of pleasure and satisfaction. I recommend it for everyone!

Assistant Church Wardens

As I mentioned earlier, Assistant Church Wardens (ACWs) are very useful in sharing your burden, and we appoint our

ACWs rather than elect them. If your church has multiple services on Sundays or at Christmas, then they are in fact invaluable in taking responsibility for being the duty CW. However, that is almost as far as it goes – it is quite hard to delegate many of the CW duties other than at services.

You don't want to have anyone as an ACW. They need to be level-headed, welcoming and conscientious, and they will need some training if they are to achieve your own standards in respect of how church services function. Ours are appointed by the APCM on recommendation by the PCC; I would never want to open this up to volunteers or to elections. I am sure you can think of people who you would never trust in this important function.

"Sidesperson" tends to be used for those people who welcome people into church at services and hand out hymn books. To distinguish them, I refer to these as "welcomers". However, in its former use, the term "Sidesman" carried some status, and in the use of the term nowadays it has lost that aura of responsibility. Hence we use the term "Assistant Church Warden" to restore something of the role that we expect them to play, i.e., to deputise for the CWs in their absence and take charge if needed.

Canon E2 is in fact entitled *Of sidesmen or assistants to the churchwardens*, and that is the only place I can find where the ACW title is used. However, do not confuse "Assistant CWs" with "Deputy CWs", who have a specific legal status which only applies in a quite limited number of cases.

9

Security And Keys

Balancing security and access for all

Sadly, the days when a parish church in town could be left open unattended are long gone. Security is a necessary evil which prevents people from accessing our churches when they would like. The threats of mindless vandalism and organised theft are too great to ignore if your church is likely to attract passing villains in a pretty market town or a city centre. You occasionally find a church apparently open and unattended, but I bet there are CCTV cameras watching!

In general, old churches were naturally very well built, which is quite logical – if they weren't, they would not have survived, would they? A structure will always have its weak points which must be identified and reinforced. With a typical church, these will usually be the doors and windows. The roof will also be a possible entry point, if access to it is available; moreover, it can itself be in danger if it utilises lead or copper, although that danger varies as the price of metals fluctuates.

Some good locks may suffice in many cases but, depending on its location, there may be a need to enlist the help of a security expert to assess the threat and make expensive recommendations accordingly. However, much can be done on a self-help basis in many cases, and a lot of security is, as with many other "expert" matters, largely a matter of common sense. You also have to be careful considering the requirements of emergency egress – it seems obvious that security requirements are often in complete conflict with the need for emergency egress, and a necessary balance has to be found.

However, I do suggest that it is possible to have too much security: at Bogthornly, our verger Dick was the sort of person that you need around the place – old and hard to understand, but willing and always there when needed. His one real fault was over-zealous security. One Sunday, the pianist decided to play the last hymn on the organ, which was in a loft above the west entrance. I think the hymn was *Guide me, O Thou Great Redeemer* or *And Can It Be?* – something that should be played in an enthusiastic fortissimo. Unfortunately, he never thought to communicate this intention to the verger. On heading to the doors at the back with the dismissal in progress just before the final hymn, he found the doors to upstairs were already locked with chain and padlock. Precisely when these had been applied was not clear – I know I always made a noise with that chain, so I don't know how Dick did it quietly during the service – but there was no option left for the would-be organist other than to return to the piano and play with gusto.

Apart from the incident with the organ, there were other humorous happenings. A few minutes after the service another week, my attention was drawn to the glazed doors by the appearance of one of the Sunday School teachers waving frantically from the far side. She had been unwise enough to return to her classroom to tidy up after the service and, trying to leave, found her way barred with the inevitable chain and padlock – the verger had struck again!

With security, you can always go too far and, personally, this sort of thing has always annoyed me. In my Royal Air Force career, it always seemed that security and lack of logic went hand in hand; being a very logical person you can understand that I was always annoyed by this sort of thing. The trick is to find the right level of security, neither too little (which is a waste of time), nor too much (which is intrusive and annoying, as well as being a waste of money).

At Anchorton – a rural village church – we held a flower festival one Saturday, at which the CW used his video camera extensively. That night, we had a break-in through the leaded stained glass window in the chancel. The miscreants left their blood on a temporary donations jar and attacked the permanent donations box (sunk in the wall) with a pickaxe, but only succeeded in scarring the surface. On reviewing the previous day's video tape, the CW's daughter recognised some unusual teenage visitors as fellow pupils at the local secondary school, and a visit from the police did the rest.

Of course, there is still a security threat even when the church is open for a service. At the same church another time, we had a wake-up when I discovered that the offering bag from the early morning communion had gone missing, together with its contents. It transpired that the choir at the later Morning Prayer service were in the habit of walking outside the church to the west door from the vestry, leaving it unlocked behind them. Some opportunist had noticed this and lifted a money bag from the desk. The only good thing was that the culprits had not realised that the safe containing some church silver was unlocked! Needless to say, the basses at the back of the procession had to carry the ancient vestry key thereafter.

At Bogthornly, a busy urban street passed by the church door, and this was quite a security and safety risk – I used to stand by the door whilst parents chatted to the vicar after the service, to catch the toddlers who would otherwise just have wandered out onto the street. During a service, the women always took their handbags up to the communion rail with them, rather than leave them unattended in the pew for a few minutes. We found that it was important to ensure that there was always a grown man standing at the back during the administration: on one occasion, a latecomer decided to try his luck with the donations box at the back (even though it was screwed to the wall), and so we always took it in turns to be the discourager of intruders. Many unknown faces peered in the main doors during services, and a friendly 'Do come and join us' with a smile often resulted in an immediate departure.

Do I have enough keys?

There is a grave danger of the CWs acting like jailers, always with a pocket bulging due to a huge bunch of keys; I have even known CWs who were proud of how large their bunch of keys was! There can easily be ten or fifteen which you need to have on you at any time, and if you include the church hall, there might be another ten or twenty. It is seriously difficult to manage that sort of number of keys, both due to the physical weight and volume of the bunch, plus also the question as to whether you can recall what each one is for.

As new churchwarden at Bogthornly, I found that the verger and the vicar each had a large bunch of keys which allowed full access everywhere, but I had very few. The verger's actions were possibly part of a power struggle, but more probably I think it was just that he didn't see why I would want to access the tower, or the classrooms, or even the doors at the back of the church which led to the galleries, organ and tower.

It was the treasurer there who gave me a really good piece of advice about keys: get a key cabinet. Ideally, this should be secured with a combination, which is easier to change than replacing the lock, and much cheaper than getting new cabinet keys for numerous people. This cabinet, securely attached to the wall, allows you to label each key and keep them centrally where they can be accessed by anyone to whom you give the combination. Then each CW just needs to keep a much smaller bunch of the frequently used keys, as holding just a few does make life much easier. (Top tip – I started to keep my own front door key on my church bunch, after I locked myself out too often.) You might wish to give certain frequently used keys to a limited number of other people according to their role, and a wider number of people should have only the necessary key or keys to get to the key box.

Then it becomes necessary to have a key register. This MUST be continuously maintained – at one church I carefully emailed my CW counterpart every time I issued a new key, only to find when he retired as CW that the list was three years out of date!

When people leave a role, you will find that they have all sorts of reasons why they should keep their keys. This can be pretty annoying and also expensive as keys are not cheap these days. However, I do advise that you should be strong and make every effort to restrict the widespread issue of keys.

You will find lots of other keys around the place. I had literally hundreds at both Bogthornly and Clamcester, and sorting them out was a mammoth task. Naturally, you don't want to throw a good key away; but on the other hand, it's pretty silly to keep a key that you know has no function. I had two keys clearly marked for particular doors in the church, but when I tried them they fitted but would not turn. I do wish that whoever had the new locks fitted had also thrown the old keys away. In this context, I recall having to force myself to recycle a set of keys that I found which belonged to a house which the church had sold two years previously – I decided that the explanations of knocking unannounced on their door to give them a set of their own house keys might be a bit embarrassing! However, the other keys at Clamcester are still there "just in case" I ever find a lock of which I was unaware – finding a home for one in such cases is a real joy! By the way, if you find that you have a mass of old brass keys (e.g., fifty keys for the old front door lock), be aware that brass has a decent value per kg at a recycling/scrap yard.

When all the keys are sorted, you should have some spares, hopefully now identified and labelled. These are valuable and should be kept safely and securely. There is no point in having a key cabinet if you then have a tin full of spare keys in the "CWs' drawer" or some other place that people go rifling through, trying to find the one they want. If you have a church office then they could be kept there – it does need to be somewhere that other people are not going to discover.

At Clamcester, we had superglue inserted into one of the padlocks on the church hall gates by an unknown person. This was pretty annoying, as there were many of these keys in circulation. It was, of course, a complete coincidence that this happened a day after a confrontation between a church member and a neighbour of the church who did not like where we left our bins on collection day. We were delighted that a person at a local key/shoe repair shop was able to procure a new padlock that used the same key. In fact, we bought a spare padlock as well, just in case it happened again.

10

People And Communications

Publicity and the Media

At some time in your career as CW, you might have some contact with the local media, most often the local newspaper but possibly a radio station or even TV. You never know when this sort of thing is likely to happen – often at just the time when you are busy and really want to be doing something else. When this occurs, you will probably find that everybody else has taken a step backwards and left you holding the baby. There is something in most British people that seems to shrink from such activities and, as I said earlier, if in doubt then it's probably the CW's job. So it helps if you have some idea of what happens.

I guess there are two types of event where a CW could get involved with the media: the first is where the church has approached the news media to, say, publicise or report an event, and the second is where the media wants to contact someone in the church about some event that they have heard of. Clearly, the first is more controllable, whereas the second can really catch you unawares. You need to know who to contact at the various media, by email and by phone, or how to find that out in a hurry.

As CW, I have been in the local newspaper on many occasions, I have been interviewed live on local radio six times and I have twice appeared on local TV (a very minor channel). Most of these have been when we wanted to tell people about events at the church or work being done to the church; just a couple of the news items were as a result of a phone call from the local paper.

There is a real skill in writing a press release, and I won't presume to tell you how, as it is not a skill I possess. Suffice it to say that if you want to get something published or advertised, you really need to find out how to write a press release, or else find someone to do it for you. Simply, though, a well-written press release will get you publicity and a poorly written one probably won't. Obviously, without a written press release, you are dependent on how the reporter interprets what you say on the phone and whether they can be bothered to follow it up. You are then reliant upon them for accuracy, and in my experience they are not noted for attention to detail, even in spelling names correctly; however, a well-written press release allows them to use chunks of it as quotations, which makes their life easier as all they have to do is to edit your piece. In particular, I have found that they prefer photographs with people (even if just lined up, but better if actually doing something) and quotations from named people (i.e., *Churchwarden Matthew Clements said…*), especially about feelings as opposed to the bare facts.

The local paper really likes a good photo opportunity. A group of people standing around looking at the camera is pretty boring, but if you have something interesting to be photographed, you might well get on the front page. If they don't send a photographer, try to take your own photos, preferably high resolution, as they won't use low definition photos. When we had some stained glass windows vandalised, one panel was almost kicked out entirely so we removed it for safety. A good photo of this clearly showing the damaged glass was the centrepiece of the front page the next week, with yours truly holding it whilst remembering to look upset rather than smiling.

Another time, we were about to conclude a major restoration project on the tower in time for Remembrance, and we had had the weather cock re-gilded. This was an impressive bird which looked magnificent covered with new gold leaf, and so several photos which I provided duly appeared, together with a lot of words taken directly from my press release, coupled with some quotes from emails. Since the press like photos with people, one photo was of the CWs with the vicar, all of us holding the cockerel. I was careful to time this release so that it appeared after the cockerel had been reinstalled – I didn't want anyone thinking they could try to steal a real gold cockerel. This item was actually published three days before Remembrance, which was also a good way of telling the town that the scaffolding was down after more than four months; I was also quite surprised by the number of people who spoke to me on the Sunday who had seen the article.

Once, the local paper called me out of the blue, asking about a funeral just held at the church. As it happened, I had acted as verger at that service so was able to provide a couple of quotations on the phone, which were duly published. Had I not been the verger, I would have promised to call them back myself with the information or, if I felt he could cope with this, I would have got the actual verger to do so. What you must never do with the media is to annoy them by not calling back – that could really cause you problems in the future, as well as effectively allowing them to publish whatever they want about the church.

Two of my radio broadcasts were done with a single person who appeared with a radio car and interviewed me at the church. The rest were done by phone from home, usually early in the morning, so I sat downstairs in my dressing gown whilst my wife listened upstairs. In preparing for a live interview by phone, I found it helpful to draw up a list of things that I wanted to say. Some of these were just a few words, others a couple of sentences. As the interview progressed, I ticked off what I had said, and I found those useful phrases were helpful in avoiding the 'err…' whilst I made my brain work at that early hour. I also made sure that I wrote down the presenter's name.

On the other hand, there was one occasion when I was pleased to make sure that the church was not mentioned in the local paper. My fellow CW took a call about a woman who had complained that some article had been stolen from her husband's grave in the churchyard; he apologised for this and said some customary platitudes. When he told me a day later, I at once realised that they must have meant the town council's cemetery adjacent to the churchyard, which is nothing to do with us. I called the contact at the paper at once to explain as the reason was undeniable: our churchyard was closed for burials in 1855, and so no one alive could possibly have a husband or wife buried there. I was quite pleased when the article appeared prominently without mentioning the church at all.

Building a relationship with the local press can pay dividends: I was most surprised a few years after the above events to get an email from the same person at the newspaper, asking if the church would like to have a monthly history slot, about 500 words with photos welcome. We were, of course, delighted to oblige, and it doesn't need much cunning to focus each article on something which is historical and yet also relates to a special service or other event at church.

Visitors and Welcoming

Welcoming visitors to the church is another of those CW jobs that I regard as essential, even though it doesn't seem to be highlighted in any of the other "churchwarden books". It has always puzzled me that the Church (in general, and not just the C of E) tries to encourage us to evangelise and get new members/believers from outside, yet many of us are apparently very bad at making regular members from the new people who voluntarily come through our doors every week.

I always regard a person who comes to a service at our church for the first time as a possible new member – okay, they might be a casual visitor with no intention of ever returning, but when they first come in you do not know that! Even then, they should leave with memories of how welcoming you all were – you have no idea how that could affect someone in the future. Even if they just call in to see the inside of the church, a short conversation can be another little step in their journey of being persuaded that we Christians are actually not odd, not really different, but just people who believe in Someone and want to share that.

At Bogthornly, I once spoke to an elderly couple who popped in one Saturday whilst I was doing some practical repair work. They had come from Australia and proudly told me that they were celebrating their 60th wedding anniversary by making a trip back to the UK for the first time in those sixty years. He had been in the Royal Australian Air Force in the Second World War and she was a local lass who had been an ack-ack gunner; they met and got married in Bogthornly as soon as the war finished, before going together to his home in Australia. Then they proudly produced a photograph of them on their wedding day, almost on the very spot where we were standing in the church. It was clearly taken in wartime as the chancel window was boarded up to prevent damage in the bombing, a fact of which I had been told, but here was proof. If I hadn't taken the time to speak to them, they might have returned home with a very different picture of where she was brought up, and I would not have been able to put such a lovely picture on the church website for six months.

In another example, as treasurer at Anchorton, I was probably the only person in the congregation apart from the vicar who knew everybody in the church – this was a deliberate policy on my part by which I kept the planned giving fairly well up to date. One evening at the PCC, we were discussing welcoming and someone claimed that we were a welcoming church where we all knew each other. I begged to differ.

'Apart from the vicar,' I said, 'who knows who Tom Smith is?' Blank looks from everyone around the table. So I described Tom and where he sat in church on about every other Sunday.

'Oh, him,' they said. 'Is that his name?' The next Sunday it seemed that there was a queue of PCC members all saying hello to Tom, who must have wondered what on earth was going on!

In my opinion, the welcoming of visitors is one of the most important roles in the church, and I consider it almost a "spiritual crime" to let unknown people come into the church and then leave without having the chance to have a conversation. You don't know who they are or why they are there – are they visitors to the area or have they come to hear their banns? Are they locals who have decided to come and see the church where they were baptised? Were they once local and have returned from miles away (such as possibly the USA or further) for a visit to see the font in which they were baptised? Have they come because they need to talk to someone about a deep spiritual problem? Have they just moved to the town and are they looking for a place to worship? You just don't know until you talk to them.

In my view, the trick to welcoming is to just have a sentence or two that will break the ice. Even just 'Hello, do you live locally or have you come far?' will get them talking as they cannot just answer 'yes' or 'no'!

Obviously, the CWs cannot do this on their own. I like to set an example in welcoming, and it is great that there are a few on whom I know I can rely, but the CWs especially need the help of the welcomers or sidespeople or whatever you call the people who stand at the door and hand out hymn books. Even then, it is surely the responsibility of every church member to welcome the stranger to the church, whether they are there for a service or have just walked in at some odd time on a weekday. Some people will volunteer to open the church; and they think that this task simply involves unlocking and doing a crossword whilst keeping an eye on people – well, it's a start, but there's a lot of untapped benefit.

Welcoming is one reason why I really do dislike it when people try to talk "church business" with me just before a service or, even worse, actually during a service, such as at the Peace. If I am on duty and the service is about to start, then I am focussing on whether everything is ready for the service and whether there are any people in church whom I do not recognise. Who are they? Why have they come? Have they been welcomed? If I have time then I certainly want to use it wisely and speak to them before the service; failing that, a quick 'welcome' at the peace or, as a last resort, I have to get between them and the door at the end. Even if I am not on duty that day, I still want to spend my time on the people who I might never see again. The last thing I want at church is to be distracted by someone asking me to remember to tell my wife something ('tell her yourself!'), or whether I can attend a meeting on Friday fortnight ('I'll need to check my calendar later'). In these days of email and text, the answer is simple: 'not now, send me (or my wife) an email or a text'; I commend this to everyone!

In the same way, whilst it is good to meet as the Body of Christ and talk with our friends, we really should make more effort to talk first with the people whom we do not know, to welcome them and to make sure they get a cup of coffee. It is said that people decide whether to buy a house within a few seconds of entering the entrance hall; in the same way, I think people decide very quickly whether to come back to a church for a second time.

At Clamcester, we have a free leaflet about the church to hand out to visitors, and this is an ideal way of breaking the ice with a visitor outside of a service (this leaflet is now available in seven languages). Sometimes you just need to find the right phrase as you say hello: I once saw two people crouching down outside near the bins and simply said, 'Are you okay down there?' An hour's discussion ensued, on a wide variety of spiritual matters. Another time, I guided four Americans around the church for an hour and received a £50 note as a donation to the church. I didn't do it for the money (although we are always grateful for the income), but I am glad to have my efforts acknowledged occasionally.

A word of caution: when I say that you should speak to visitors, there are pitfalls. When we were looking for a church once, on our first Sunday in our new home, we went into a nearby church for the Sunday service. It was a bit high for us, with several acolytes/servers dressed in white, but the welcome at the door was fine and it was a decent-sized congregation. Then, during the Peace, the chap I had identified as the duty CW asked if we would be willing to take the elements down with the offertory. I found this quite surprising and declined, saying that as it was our first visit, we didn't know how things were done here. My personal thought was that if the CW doesn't know which people in the congregation are first-time visitors, then the fellowship here must be fairly superficial. On a subsequent Sunday, we went to the other extreme:

a charismatic Anglican church with a vibrant and good-sized congregation (albeit mostly much younger than us). It should have been a great experience, but there are many things about that church service still etched in my memory for the wrong reasons, such as too many "in-jokes" which we couldn't understand. The one that really stands out even now was the Peace, which seemed to be treated as "The Intermission", where everyone got up and spent ten minutes or more talking to their friends. Knowing no one, we remained in our pew, and in all that time just one young woman came and welcomed us. After the service finished we found that, as visitors, we were expected to make ourselves known at the "Welcome table". We quietly left instead, never to return.

Safeguarding

Safeguarding is now, sadly, an essential part of how churches and many other organisations have to be run. Like it or not, it is important, and the rules have to be followed; they are there for your protection as much as that of vulnerable children and adults. Your church should already have a safeguarding officer, and there will be training at various levels required for certain people, guidance to be followed and forms to be filled in. This all needs doing, and if your church doesn't do it then I suggest you urgently speak to the safeguarding officer at the diocese for advice. Note that I am NOT suggesting that this is a job for a CW – you are (or should be) far too busy to take on this as well.

In writing this, I am shocked to realise that I have knowledge of four totally separate legal cases involving child abuse, one through my work and three through different churches that I attended. As I look back at those (one was thirty years ago), I see how both my views and the law have changed; fortunately, our awareness has also increased and, hopefully, the church is a safer place than it was. It does seem that the church has moved from one crisis to another to another, and I think it sad that such matters continue to detract from our mission and purpose.

A safeguarding officer I know was helping the diocese by visiting churches to educate them about safeguarding. At one church she was shocked when confronted with almost the entire PCC whose unanimous view was that 'none of this applies to us, we don't have any children here and we're only here tonight because we were told we had to come.' I am sure that many other churches like this exist throughout the country – when it comes to the law of the land we must all understand that, no matter how we might dislike it, it applies to us all. If it is stated that your role in the church requires a DBS check, then that must be obtained; if there is training applicable to your role then it should be done. The earlier "one size fits all" approach has been superseded by a set of training levels which are specific to each role.

However, having said that, I do feel that the rules may sometimes hinder our contact with others, which is a pity. This is a true story which I wrote down the day it happened in church after the service some years ago, and I quote it in full exactly as originally written, other than changing the names:

Little Sophia (aged just < 2 yrs) reached up and took a biscuit from the tray on the table. I was chatting with Sade nearby and, as Sophia took a step away with her *prize, I knelt down and said, 'We saw you' to her. As I stood up, she looked up at me through her glasses and said, 'You're funny!'*

I related this to her mother who looked surprised and said, 'But she doesn't really talk! All she says is "Hello" and "Goodbye".'

Sade said, 'Well, she does now.'

Now, I am not saying that this sort of exchange cannot happen under safeguarding rules – after all, coffee time after a service is a time for sharing, welcoming and simply being friends. However, you do not need a DBS check to say three words to a small child in the proximity of her mother, and those who say that you do are simply wrong. Sadly, all too often we might feel inhibited by the knowledge of such rules, and we allow our behaviour to be constrained by them to our own loss.

It has been proven to me, many times over, that I do have some sort of ministry in respect of welcoming parents through their children. I can smile at them and get a broad grin in return, even from a tiny baby. I consider that, by showing interest in their child and getting a response, in some way I am welcoming the whole family to the church and making them feel that they are part of the wider church family.

As CW at Bogthornly, I always sat at the back. The row in front of me was where an African woman named Claudia sat with her two children, and I always greeted her when she came in. When she had a third, it became a habit that when she sat down holding her baby, I would greet her and say 'Hello' to baby Leonie at the same time. Once, she had an issue in the service with one of the older ones and, turning to me, she passed over Leonie so that she could concentrate on the matter in hand. I was quite proud that an older white male could be trusted without thought to look after her baby! Later, when Leonie was about two years old, she once or twice walked down to the communion rail with me and after the administration willingly took my hand to walk back up the aisle together.

Interactions like these are a fundamental part of our faith. Clearly, there is a fine line here – the time and place were appropriate, and the mothers knew me well. We should all get on so well that we will trust each other in this way and not allow rules to interfere with what is meant to be "normal" and in fact is another way of showing the love of Christ to others.

Data Protection

Data protection, in the guise of the *General Data Protection Regulation (GDPR)*, has suddenly appeared as the latest thing to bother all of us. It is actually a regulation in EU law (Number 2016/679) which covers data protection and privacy for all individuals within the European Union.

At first glance, it seems almost overpowering in its scope but, when analysed, it should be seen as a welcome marker in the sand as we move forward in the 21st century. It is pretty clear that there are a few enormous companies in the world who have all sorts of power as they know so much about each of us. In fact, some of the companies could be likened to the corporations run by certain Bond villains; those stories seemed far-fetched when they came out, but suddenly we are seeing how prescient they are. Knowledge is power or rather, in modern terms, data is power.

Any laws which inhibit the ability of unknown people and corporations to know about me are, in my view, only too welcome. I have no presence on Facebook or Twitter, for instance, and I refuse all suggestions to complete forms online when they are asking for data about me which are nothing to do with what I am doing online. I recommend this approach as the minimum that we should all do; if something online is free, then ask yourself *What does the supplier get out of this?* Invariably, the answer is that they get data, so that they can build a picture of you and me and everyone else, because that gives them power – the power to target advertising, to present you with "fake news", to influence you – all of these help them to make more and more money, so that they can influence us all further. The GPDR is all about legislating to stop some of these practices, so believe me; it's worth complying with it.

At the time of writing, the precise implications of GPDR are still being worked out, as EU regulation is understandably written in some sort of foreign language which almost no one speaks fluently – well, perhaps lawyers do (or pretend they do, as that's how they make money!). Too many people (especially the UK media) like to take a phrase in an EU regulation and find some extreme interpretation just to make some scare headline; in fact, I think that's a particularly British characteristic which is, frankly, pretty sad.

I think as far as churches are concerned, you need to get someone to take this on, preferably not a CW. If you (the church) can then craft a Data Privacy Notice which covers what the church wants to do with knowledge of their name, address, phone number and email, then getting that signed by each member should cover the church nicely. In my view, a name only is not covered by GPDR – it has to be a set of data which links something else to your name.

Volunteers

Churches are largely run by volunteers. It is perhaps obvious but I should point out the meaning of the word "volunteer". They are not paid, but nevertheless willingly take on great responsibility, and without them most churches would cease to function. Some volunteers are ministers (ordained or lay); many others are just conscientious people who want to help the church to live, and possibly even live abundantly. They don't have to do it; we should never forget that volunteers can change their mind at any time and simply walk away if they so choose.

Many people will volunteer to do something, even without any public request for help such as an announcement in church. Others will happily respond when there is such a public request, but there will still be others who need to be asked even though an appeal was made for volunteers. Spotting people who appear to have talents but are hardly involved in church activities is perhaps a talent in itself; nevertheless, I commend it to CWs. A direct suggestion to a suitable person has so often resulted in them gladly agreeing to help, saying, 'I didn't want to put myself forward; I was waiting to be asked.'

Just consider the list of tasks and roles (in no particular order) that are filled by volunteers in any C of E church: lay minister, churchwarden, treasurer, secretary, PCC member, sacristan, choir member, music group member, flower arranger, bell-ringer, sidesperson, coffee-making, event-running, church cleaner, visitor of the sick and elderly, members of many committees, Eucharistic assistant, crucifer, grass cutter, general maintenance dogsbody, brass cleaner, linen washer/ironer, reader, Sunday School teacher (or equivalent), youth club leader, house group leader… The list is effectively endless and of course one individual can fulfil many of these roles.

But the volunteers do far more than those tasks. Try this quick test. In your church, do you know:

- Who puts the bins out?
- Who brings then back in again?
- Who cleans the toilets?
- Who buys more loo paper?
- Who replaces a broken light bulb?
- Who reads the gas and electricity meters?
- Who sets the heating timer for the week's events?
- Who put down some salt outside the door when it last snowed?
- Who counts the collections and pays the cash into the bank?
- Who organises the annual check of the fire extinguishers?
- Who buys the gluten-free wafers?
- Who cleans the chalice after a service?
- Who sets the church clock forward in March and back in October?
- Who turns the page on the Book of Remembrance?

I'm sure you can think of your own questions along the same lines. Try thinking of the odd little jobs around the place – someone has to do them, often frequently, perhaps once or more every week. Identify several for which you don't know the answer, and then try to find the answer. You might just be surprised at what you find out about other people – whether it is that you didn't know people had been doing something for years, or whether just one or two people just do so many more things than you were aware of. Then consider that some people also do a lot more besides of which you are still not aware – the hidden things that happen under the surface, invisible to most, routinely done without complaint.

Now stop and think: do we in the Church of England look after our volunteers as we should? Do we even know what they all do? Do we ever thank them or even acknowledge their contribution? How much would they be missed if more than one left at the same time!

I am sure that most volunteers do what they do out of love for God. Possibly my favourite verse is Matthew ch 5, v 16: *Let your light so shine before men [and women] that they may see your good works and give glory to your Father in heaven.* We don't do things in order to achieve our salvation (as that's a free gift), but we should do good works precisely because we are already saved through grace. Equally, we don't do good work to make us more acceptable to God, because we know that we cannot do anything at all to make God love us more or less than He does already. We are not after the gratitude of men and women, because we know that God sees what we do and that is enough.

Mind you, we are only human, and so a little thanks occasionally does indeed go an awfully long way!

Vacancies and Selection

Oh, what fun! A vacancy. Now what?

A lot goes through your head when the vicar announces that she is leaving. Well, if she's at all kind, she will tell the CWs in confidence first, before telling the PCC and announcing it to the congregation. She may either be retiring, in which case she will choose her departure date, or else she is going to a new parish, in which case that date has been (or is about to be) agreed with the new parish. Either way, you have very little say in that. Probably your immediate reaction will be to want to find out how soon a replacement will be forthcoming, but the answer really is "How long is a piece of string?" The bishop told the departing incumbent at Clamcester that it would be a short interregnum, but it wasn't; if you are told this, do not put any bets on the length!

Without doubt, a vacancy is when the CWs really earn their keep. This is when you find all sorts of things that the vicar did which you had no idea about, you discover lots of items which cause you pain and pressure, and you appreciate for the first time just how much stress the vicar has been under, day in, day out, for years.

Having got over the initial shock of the announcement (which might well come totally out of the blue) and asked the question "when will the new vicar get here?", I think the next question is then "what is the process for a replacement going to be?" I know that I am quite process driven but believe me, in this sort of situation you really will want to know just what is going to happen and when, what needs to be done and precisely how much of it is down to the CWs.

However (and it still seems strange to me), at the time of our vacancy, no one could tell me what the process would be; I had imagined that the diocese would have to cope with probably fifty vacancies per year, and since the diocese has been around for a good long time, the path would be pretty well trodden and clear to follow. Not so, it seems. There is a diocesan employee whose role is to advise the parish on these matters, but it took us some while to get a meeting set up. Then when it did happen I was asked bluntly, 'What's your hurry?' Later on, all became clear when it was announced that the adviser had a month's sabbatical and then was getting promoted within the diocese, leaving the adviser post vacant for a while. Had I not pushed for that meeting, we would have been delayed at least an additional three months, in an interregnum that lasted fourteen months even with my pushing.

The first thing that the parish has to do is to produce a parish profile. This forms the basis of the advertisement and so has to "sell" the parish to the applicants. Despite the selling aspect, the profile must not simply promote the current glowing situation and ignore the real issues which exist; obviously, you still want to attract applicants, but telling lies about the place does no one any favours. People like to overstate the positives and gloss over the negatives, but you need to be clear about the challenges and the scope for achievement for the new vicar. Hopefully, most dioceses now have a good template with a realistic description of what is meant to go in it; at the time of our vacancy, the template for the Diocese of Clamcester was not fit for purpose, with many fundamental issues which we had to fight around. We wondered how they had been doing any recruiting at all with such an awful document as a guide. Eventually, we managed to produce a very large profile which did all that was necessary according to the guide, and then we had to spend a while cutting it down to a sensible size. The effort of all this was considerable for a good number of people.

Getting the advertisement approved and published and giving potential applicants time to apply all takes time. Then there will be some weeks until the interview panel can agree a suitable date; it all adds up. In our case, I think it was the bishop who did a first cull of the applications, sifting out the people who were not even qualified to do the job; one of these was actually from a minister in a different denomination who tried to justify to the bishop how he could do the job without being a priest in the C of E! Then you move to the selection for interview stage, at which the selection panel (which would probably include both CWs) has to read through each application and try to score each applicant. Some of this was difficult: we had one from someone called "Chris" and we couldn't even work out if this was a male or female. Another told us very little about himself, but we did learn the name of his pet parrot. Some were easy: one spelt the name of the church wrongly several times and also told us how his plans for next year included both climbing Mount Kilimanjaro and writing a book – if that was his view of how life would be in this busy parish, he was very much mistaken!

The interviews are interesting: there might be a priest who is in the diocese already but probably needs a move and so has been persuaded to apply by the bishop – you might call her the "bishop's favourite". You need to be fair with this sort of applicant; but in our case, she performed very badly both with her short sermon and in the interview, so we had no real problem in discounting her in favour of the eventual appointee. You then have to wait to announce it, as the new appointee must tell her present parish before it goes public. This is usually followed by a three-month wait, which is the notice period for her current parish. There is still more waiting as it is unlikely that your preferred day for the service of induction and institution is possible for the bishop's busy timetable (but do try to fix this date immediately after the appointment). Then, at last, after the service of induction and institution, you are free – well, almost; now the proper job begins, as you get to know the new vicar and learn to work with her.

Whilst all this has been going on, there has been a parish to run, and the CWs have been doing it. It is no one else's responsibility; it is the CWs who do it. Some people might expect to take over, such as the curate or any other priest that the parish has, but this is not the situation. The curate, the associate ministers and the LLMs are all there to assist the CWs, not the other way round. This is where you find out just what pressures the vicar has to bear constantly – the many calls on his time, the unjust criticisms, the silly questions and the burdensome and distracting issues, all draining your energy and diverting you from the task.

A vacancy is certainly one time when the abilities to lead a team and to delegate will stand you in good stead; the CWs cannot do it all themselves. One of the real pains of a vacancy is that the CWs have to look after the vicarage, unless the diocese has managed to let it for the duration.

If you have any influence, try to get them to do this, as it will bring them income and save you work.

I have to say that I can see no good reason for not being able to start the entire process whilst the previous incumbent is still in post, other than to save a few months' stipend in the diocesan budget. It seems to me that the process takes advantage of the volunteer CWs who get no reward in this life for flogging themselves to death for a year longer than needed. If the process was timed so that the interviews were planned to be on (or very soon after) the existing incumbent's last day, then you could appoint very quickly and then wait for just the three months' notice period, with the service of induction and institution in the first week following. It would just take a small amount of planning, wouldn't it? Okay, I know this is the C of E...

The Notices

There are two types of notice in a church: the sort you pin on a board and the sort that you give out at the end of a service. Both are liable to cause some stress, for different reasons.

I have found that, if left unregulated, notices will just appear on the boards in the church, causing clutter and untidiness. Getting rid of out-of-date notices promptly is essential, and it is rare that anyone other than a CW will do this – certainly, the odd people who fly-post will not do it. An old but still relevant notice with curled edges and lots of holes in each corner is a bit more problematic – you need to hand it to the person most likely involved and gently ask for a fresh version. The real bugbear for me is the unauthorised notices which just appear – a concert is held in church and a few days later you notice a pile of flyers for a concert to be held somewhere else, left by the hirers; or it might be an advertising flyer for a commercial product. I'm sorry, but these notices go straight into the recycling bin, and I encourage you to do the same. The only ones that I will tolerate are for events in the church or the hall, and even then the purely commercial ones do not belong in church.

This is, of course, a matter of personal like and dislike. There are no rules about such things but, I am sure, if you don't exercise some control then there will be so many that most people would never look at them at all.

When it comes to giving notices at a church service, I am convinced that many people just do not listen. You have to keep the list of announcements as short and succinct as possible; if there is a notice sheet of any sort, then try very hard to not repeat any of them, although it will often be necessary to highlight one or two. Having several people all come to the front to give their notice is an invitation for verbosity and boredom, so I only very rarely allow that – only on the few occasions where I think that they can explain it better than me. I also ensure that we have some sort of understanding as to how long they can talk for – I recall vividly one person being allowed by the vicar to give a notice which went on for almost fifteen minutes (and that was after a one-hour-and-forty-minute service!). The other thing to watch out for is someone sneaking up whilst you are giving your brief notices and the first you know is when they ask you, in public, whether they can give a notice as well. You can hardly say 'No,' but I make sure they never try that again!

I do think that I can claim to have given three notices that people still remember, because that is very easy when you have a good visual aid. The first occasion was when a repair job was being done to a parapet wall on the church roof; this wall was in a worse state than we had realised previously and had been in danger of collapsing due to the stone being weakened. Sensing an opportunity to communicate, I wore my workman's rubber gloves and held a piece of removed stone in each hand, whilst my wife held a bucket underneath. I said, 'This is why we are doing this job on the roof,' and rubbed the two pieces of stone together – they satisfyingly crumbled into grey sand!

The second one was on a later job when the stone finials on top of the tower pinnacles were being replaced. I had the sole remaining finial and showed the congregation its worn condition, and then we showed on the screen a picture of the new finial in place, looking superb. So far, so good. Then I gently put the old finial down on the floor and a piece broke off, to general amusement. Well, at least it proved the point.

The third one was also in relation to the works on the tower. I have already mentioned the weather vane in the shape of a cockerel (about two feet high) which was re-gilded with gold leaf. People certainly looked at that when I held it up, the day before it was to be reinstalled, and they were keen after the service to take photos of it being held by their children!

If there is genuinely no need for notices then I am always keen to tell the vicar beforehand, just to demonstrate that I don't want to stand up there for no real purpose. Of course, you might never be asked to give a notice in church as your vicar might ban the practice entirely. That view is probably based on the misconception that people will both take home and read the notice sheet; this is not my experience! The vicar could also extend the ban to having no notices at all on display in church, but this might lead to some difficulties in communication. However, I have to say that I have never been in such a church where both these were enforced.

11

Money Matters

Accounting Concepts and Definitions

It might not surprise you to know that there are some rules for accounting, but you might be surprised to know that these were introduced as recently as 1997 – prior to that there were no rules and no standards, so everyone did the best they could (or, rather, they did exactly what they wanted to, usually based on their predecessor's method). The accounting rules are currently known as "The Charities Act 2011 and the PCC" (*The Rules*), and include a fair bit that every PCC member needs to know. Incidentally, I was told once that the original Charities Act in 1993 (and hence the first edition of *The Rules* in 1997) was brought about because a certain large national charity was the victim of a seven-figure fraud which was made possible because of their lack of financial controls; this showed the government how lax the charity law was in this respect.

As CW, you don't need to be an accountant, but you do need to have some idea of the concepts in *The Rules*. If the accounts are to have any value, then they must not only be accurate but also consistent (which I believe are the two most important of the basic accounting principles). "Consistent" means that the accounts are worked out on the same principles each year or, if not, then the differences are clearly stated. If the treasurer doesn't understand the rules then he is liable to do things differently each year, which makes year-on-year comparisons meaningless.

A definition that needs to be understood is "what money should the PCC account for?" This is such an important question that there is a whole chapter near the start of *The Rules* which clarifies the responsibilities of the PCC for accounting. You might think that it is simply answered but it's not that easy. Essentially, the PCC has to account for the money that it controls, i.e., where the PCC can decide how it is spent. At one church I have attended, the annual accounts included several things as income which weren't, such as the fees received and forwarded to the diocese, funeral collections for Cancer Research or the "income" for the church pilgrimage; none of these were controlled by the PCC. By including things such as these, the church income was being wildly overstated (which, if your parish share is based partly on income, might actually be costing your church money). I invented the term "non-income" to cover these items which the PCC does not control; although such transactions are on our financial database, by definition they should sum to zero each year. Just because they have been through the church bank account does not make them reportable.

Concepts like "Restricted Funds" are important for all PCC members (as trustees) to understand – not just the CWs. If all PCC members are clear about this, it will make financial discussions much easier. My wife once worked at a national charity where she had an argument with a couple of millionaire trustees who thought that they could spend a Restricted donation for a project in whatever way they chose, because they had decided not to complete that particular project in order to save money and spend it elsewhere! That option does not exist for Restricted money.

Annual Report and Accounts

The Annual Report for the church is two things: a written report on activities, which must cover various essential details, and the financial accounts. In some cases it seems that the treasurer has to do the Annual Report rather than the secretary, presumably because he has to do the financial bit.

By the way, the APCM has to be held between March 1ˢᵗ and April 30ᵗʰ. At Anchorton, the habit was to hold this meeting as soon as possible in March and this put a huge strain on the treasurer to prepare the accounts and get them examined quickly. It also means that a new CW can be elected and not actually take up his post for three months. Therefore, it makes a lot more sense to hold the APCM in the middle of April as this eases both of these issues, and so I got that changed as soon as I could.

Apart from the treasurer, at least one other person in the church should be familiar with this publication; not only can she be ready to offer advice and assistance to the treasurer but can also give assurance to the PCC (as trustees) about the state of the accounts, as there will be very few people on the PCC who are that interested. The key point is that this person should NOT be the vicar, even if he used to be an accountant! (In fact, if that is the case, it is even more important that he is not involved, as his knowledge is certain to be out of date and not to be relied upon – you can guess how I know.) Hence, I think it is good if one or both CWs are able to fill this function, which spreads the burden and might make it easier for you to find a volunteer treasurer who then knows he will not be alone.

The activities of the PCC in the annual report are a defined set of headings in *The Rules*; they are NOT the chatty reports of the people who do the flowers and the list of those who helped in the crèche or sang in the choir (etc.). Rather, they include the legally required details of members, policies and such things as are required by the CC and specified in *The Rules*. If your APCM wants a chatty list of who did what in the year, and where the church outing went to, that's fine, they can have one, but it's not the report that the CC wants, so it should not be called the Annual Report, nor is it the one that you should upload to the CC website (although I am sure lots of churches do).

It's also important to note that the Annual Report and accounts should relate to the financial year ending on December 31st, and not the year up to the APCM, nor the year ending April 5th. This date is set legally and cannot be changed. In practice, of course, no one will care if the text mentions things that happened a couple of weeks before the APCM, but it is essential that the figures in the accounts are for the previous calendar year. This can cause confusion about the 2018 APCM approving the 2017 Annual Report, as some think that the report presented to the 2018 APCM has to be called the 2018 Annual Report...

The Annual Report has to be approved by the APCM and a copy submitted to the CC by a set date (see "Regular Returns" below); the annual accounts also need to be uploaded as the "Financial Return" (to the C of E). To make doing the "Financial Return" easy, the accounts need to be done correctly with the right data under the right heading; it is worth checking the required format for that return so that the correct headings are used for data (if they are not already), as this return is not a copy but rather each total figure has to be entered manually. This return is the means by which the C of E issues interesting, up-to-date press releases about national church financial matters.

Just because the diocese and the CC are sent details of the accounts does not imply any sort of approval of them. Neither body has the personnel or the requirement to do any actual assessment of the quality of the accounts – all they do is check if something called by that name has been received. It would be a very conscientious Archdeacon or Area Dean who actually looked at them. My view is that the annual accounts should be as brief as possible whilst complying with "The Rules", by aggregating rows to agree with the financial return (which is quite brief). If you want to present a more detailed set of management accounts to the PCC or the congregation then I would say that is probably a good thing, but just get the APCM to approve the legally required version for submission. In the same way, the text of the Annual Report should meet the requirements of "The Rules", without going into huge detail. One of the charities of which I became treasurer (turnover c.£50,000) had an earlier report so detailed that it actually listed (for example) all twelve separate monthly payments of interest from the bank, total £17.98!

It is good for PCC members to be able to look at a set of accounts and find the important figures, such as the unrestricted surplus or deficit. If you can also pick out any figures which look unusual and question them, then you are performing a useful and valid role as a trustee. However, if you do find odd things, then I suggest you discuss them with the treasurer before the meeting as otherwise even just raising the question at the meeting can sound like public criticism. In all probability, it will be your understanding which is at fault.

As CW, I have a plastic wallet containing several documents; I take this wallet to nearly all committee meetings I attend, as any of the items might be useful for quick reference. One of these items is a copy of the previous year's accounts, and this is the most used item in that wallet. Again, I commend that practice.

Bank Account Signatories

I have served over twenty years on three different PCCs with five different vicars and probably over one hundred different PCC members. All these PCCs had one thing in common – every member seemed to think that they had no responsibility for the money! When I was treasurer at Anchorton, in PCC meetings the vicar would say 'Now Item five: finance, Matthew?' and everyone would put down their pens and take out their metaphorical (or, in one case, literal) knitting! When I pointed out that all I did was to count it and they all had collective responsibility for how we spent it, the reply I had was, 'But we trust you, Matthew.' It's nice to be trusted, but I'd prefer that people understood their own responsibilities and paid attention to financial matters. Many churches are now registered charities and PCC members are the charity's trustees; the CC website clearly specifies what their legal duties are, and these need to be brought to the attention of all members.

There is just one important rule for signing cheques – never sign blank ones! Every charity should always require dual authorisation on all external transactions (whether cheques or online), and anyone who signs even one blank cheque should be relieved of that responsibility forthwith. The few times I have signed a cheque which was not completely filled in was when the payee was already written in but we were not sure of the exact amount, or vice versa; the amount was written in but we needed to clarify the correct payee name – in such situations I felt I could trust the treasurer. The church needs to have sufficient signatories so that there is never a need for a holidaying signatory to sign a set of blank cheques before he departs for a fortnight.

In my view, it is completely wrong for the vicar to be signatory to the bank accounts – it is simply not his job, although it is permitted. I despair when I hear of a minister being convicted of theft from church funds – he should never have been allowed near them. It appears that some vicars do regard it as part of their job for some reason, but I urge you to resist this; it might be quite a battle. If you have several signatories of which one is the vicar, then just don't ever ask him to sign a cheque, and under no circumstances let him have a church cheque book. There have been regular cases of treasurers or even vicars being found guilty of some form of embezzlement of church funds, and invariably the cause was that either they had sole control of the money or that the second signatory allowed themselves to be bullied into signing blank or unsupported cheques.

In the same way, when I was treasurer at Anchorton, my wife became CW, but she was never authorised as signatory until I handed over the treasurer job; it seemed fundamentally incorrect to have husband and wife both being authorised signatories, so I never even suggested it. At my current church, we now have five signatories, with any two to sign, and it's the same signatories for all accounts – if they can be trusted for one then they can be trusted for them all, and it does make things so much easier to remember.

Online Banking

Most banks can now offer online banking with a process for two people to authorise each transaction, and I recommend this as it really does save time. It's only when you set up the week's transactions and send out an email request to the other signatories in minutes that you realise how much time was previously spent in the old-fashioned way; you have to write cheques, get a counter-signature and then pass the cheque on or post it to the recipient, and possibly type a letter as well. Most companies now give bank details for payments; just be aware of the email scam where a scammer sends an email pretending to be (say) a contractor, saying that their bank details have changed, and asking for a bill to be paid to it. This is possible if they have also hacked your emails, and so never believe such emails without checking with your contractor. A contractor I know did actually change his company bank details and then had to call all his customers to persuade them that the change was genuine! Equally, you might have to pay a new person a large sum (for instance, the first payment on a building contract), in which case you should first transfer a small amount and check that it has been received by the right party, before paying the full amount. Don't feel that this is silly – it is a wise precaution that might save your neck one day.

Counting Collections

Who counts the collection in your church? Most importantly, how many people do it each week? It should be two people. I was once the independent examiner of a church for three years – I did their accounts and their treasurer did ours (I don't think I could do that now as the required qualifications for examiners have been increased). Each year, I observed that on most Sundays only one person signed for counting the money; sometimes there was no signature and very occasionally there were two. Sadly, however, all too often the sole signature was the vicar's, and no matter how much I pointed this out, it never changed. It is not the vicar's job!

When I arrived at Clamcester, only one person did the counting, and that person was decided by the last two or three responsible people to leave the church – usually two CWs and the treasurer or secretary. The chosen person then took the cash home and counted it that afternoon. I went along with this for a while, but felt I had to revise the old form on which we entered the data as it was so much out of date. Then I made that form into an Excel spreadsheet, which then became a Workbook with two sheets, one for the paying-in, linked to the other which was where the counted amounts were entered for each item. This improved the speed of the task as well as the accuracy, and we now have a rota of seven pairs who take it in turns to count and pay in each week. When we devised the rota and included new people counting, it was easy to persuade them that this was the process. Sadly, however, one of the original counters still insisted on doing it manually for several years. Baffling.

Annual Returns

There are various returns that need to be made, mostly online, and some of them are important annual ones. Normally, these can be made by different people, including the treasurer, and the jobs do not need to fall to a CW. These returns include:

- Finance return to C of E
- Mission statistics return to C of E
- Annual Report (including accounts) to CC
- Annual update of trustee information held by CC
- Corporation Tax return (some churches)

I have been doing all of the above myself, partly because of there being no obvious alternative candidate; having ceased to be CW I am now handing this over, although there is a case that having learned how to do it, doing it again is easier than trying to train someone else! Nevertheless, I would encourage you to delegate where possible.

There seems to be a feeling in several churches that the finance and mission returns are optional, and sometimes they are not completed. The C of E uses these data for a variety of purposes, sometimes reported in the national press, and it is a shame that some churches do not care to cooperate. The mission return gives the C of E data for press releases about, say, the national number of attendees at Christmas or Easter. The issue I have had with the mission return is that this should be the responsibility of the vicar or someone delegated by him, yet the Diocese of Anchorton always sent it to me as treasurer as they knew the vicar would never do it! I once asked them, 'Am I my vicar's keeper?'!

Another time, I was so confused by the wording of some of the "mission statistics" return that I sent an email to Church House about it. This provoked an interesting discussion with the Head of Statistics for the C of E and I was thanked for my input. Some gratifying changes were made to the form the next year (such as a better definition of the four weeks for the October attendance) and I wrote again, thanking them for doing this. From the reply, I had the feeling that many people complain about these things to their friends, but few actually make helpful suggestions to Church House.

One thing about the 'mission statistics' return is the question about the "October Attendance". This is not simply a set of figures extracted from the service register but a more detailed question about how many *different* people attend church in each week of that four-week period. You should only count each person once per week, even if they attend a service every day. To be of any value, this sort of information needs to be gathered at the time, not six months later, so for that month I left a form with the service register asking for some intelligent number. The online guidance notes help considerably.

The CC need to receive a copy of the annual report within ten months of the year-end, i.e., by 31st October (given that the year-end must be 31st December). Since these are approved by the APCM, and the APCM has to be held by 30th April, there really is no excuse for not sending this off in May or June. Be aware that the CC website gives some prominence to the date that the report is received, as they consider (rightly or wrongly) that sending your return on the last possible day each year (or even later) might say something about the attitude to compliance which your charity has. If you are always doing it at the last minute and are also looking to apply for grants (e.g., for a reordering project), you might find that poor compliance could be one of the things you are scored down on.

At the same time as sending off the Annual Report to the CC, the financial return can also now be completed. Again, there is no reason for failing to submit this return soon after approval by the APCM, although I once had to point out to the diocese that it was not possible to submit it before the APCM as they had requested! This return is not necessarily done by the CW, but you should make sure that the treasurer or someone else does do it. If your accounts have been prepared in the correct format under the correct headings, then this return is very straightforward. If, however, the treasurer has ignored the guidance and done the accounts his own way, then there might well be a good deal of work still to do. Hence, if the treasurer has to do the finance return, there is more chance that he will change his system next year and do the accounts properly.

Corporation Tax is an odd one. It's one of those where you are sure that you don't have to pay anything, but confirming this is difficult. I could not understand why we had to do one, and eventually I managed to get them to stop asking us – possibly they might ask us now every five years. Perhaps they have now improved matters, but it really bugged me for some time. It also bugged a predecessor who used to log on to make a payment of £0.01 just to please them. Sadly, he died suddenly, and I had great trouble getting this responsibility transferred to my name until fortunately his widow came up with his password. These systems are all very well, but don't they consider this sort of thing in the design?

As I said before, you as CW do not have to do the above things yourself, but you need to make sure that others are doing these things. In the absence of any suitable and willing volunteer, you will of course find yourself doing them.

Budget

The church must have a budget every financial year. It is not an optional item! The budget, once approved, is the means by which the treasurer has the authority to spend money, up to the amount specified under any heading. In some categories, the PCC should decide to impose a limit on any single item of expenditure so that, for instance, the vicar cannot go and spend the year's budget in May on one expensive item of equipment. All items above that limit will need to be approved specifically by the PCC, but clearly the PCC will not wish to have to authorise every single expenditure such as direct debit payments for gas and electricity. Without a budget, the treasurer has no authority and would have to go to the PCC for every individual item of expenditure, which would bore the PCC members more than normal.

Legally, the PCC should approve the budget for Year 2 before the end of Year 1, as otherwise no payments can be made in Year 2 until this has been done. Of course, no one is that strict, but it does make sense to approve an initial budget in November and then for the PCC to approve an improved version as soon as the Year 1 figures are known.

The expenditure and income through the year should be checked against the budget at least quarterly by the PCC, or even monthly if your income is very high. The treasurer should make allowances for items that are paid annually or over ten months, or are seasonal such as heating bills. The interesting figures are the ones that should be probably roughly the same every month, such as loose plate giving or vicar's expenses; sudden spikes or dips in these are always worth investigation. The six-month figures are particularly useful as anyone should be able to understand the significance of large variations from the budgeted income or expenditure at that stage of the year. If your budget is even just vaguely correct, then a figure of 35% or 65% at that halfway stage may be giving forewarning of an issue or identifying an error.

Expenses

Once approved, the church budget (as mentioned above) is the authority for the treasurer to pay, on receipt of an invoice or receipt, for expenses made in accordance with that budget. This is how the trustees (i.e., PCC members) exercise their financial responsibilities. The church will have lots of expenses, and there is no suggestion that anyone – especially the CW – should pay for valid expenditure out of their own pocket without being able to reclaim that expense.

Of course, some individuals may feel that their own income is so good that they don't need to reclaim expenses, or they just want to donate, say, the weekly flowers, but even then there is a good reason why they should reclaim it if they pay tax: if they do not want repayment, then they should reclaim the cash and make a separate Gift Aid donation for an identical sum to the church. This means that the church will benefit by an extra 25% of the expense, which seems a no-brainer to me.

The treasurer should require that expenses are claimed frequently – people should not be allowed to build up a huge pile of receipts and submit it once per year. The vicar at Bogthornly had this problem – he would defer the job of doing his expenses for so long that it then eventually took him several days to sort out, whereas the odd half-hour every month would have been far more efficient. I once had to tell him, after being given a whole year's worth in one go:

1. You cannot afford, with your small stipend and large family, to be owed over £1,000 by the church.
2. It makes the church accounts more difficult.
3. After so long, you are bound to have forgotten expenses and lost receipts.
4. Equally, after so long, how can I approve them with any certainty?

At Clamcester, we had a paid administrator and, after about three years, I realised that she was using her own credit card to make church purchases online. I regard that as wrong, as I don't consider that it should be part of a paid employee's job, so I took it upon myself to make purchases online so long as she sent me the link. I didn't want to take on the responsibility for a church credit card, but you might think that worthwhile if there are several purchases each month.

Another time, at Bogthornly, the curate submitted a claim which included the four-week bus pass for each of the previous three months, even though the curate had just been off sick for six weeks. In the face of some opposition, I declined to approve that claim until at least the cost of one pass had been deleted. Somehow the curate had gained the impression that the church paid, regardless, for travel expenses which were not incurred in doing the job – perhaps something else omitted from training.

At one church, the PCC voted to introduce limits linking spending amounts with the number of quotations; I think it was that between £500 and £1,000, two quotations were required, and anything over £1,000 required three quotations. I voted against this as it was a blanket coverage which would only hinder me – it is hard enough to get a single quotation for specialist work such as checking the lightning conductor, so needing two quotations would ensure that the work was never done. I think that a distinction has to be made between simple items, such as purchasing something readily available from a variety of sources (such as AV equipment, chairs, books), and hard-to-find specialist contractor tasks, which include most minor work on the building. Clearly, major work has to go out to tender, but try not to let yourself get restricted too much.

Once, I was not present at a PCC meeting but had asked for £508 to be approved for something. I was smilingly informed afterwards that my request had been turned down as it was above our £500 single tender limit "and we know that you wouldn't want to bend the rules." My response was to ask the PCC by email for ex-committee approval to spend £499, saying that I would pay the other £9 myself.

One little sting in the tail that I ought to mention: it is now allowable to pay the treasurer, so it doesn't have to be an unpaid volunteer from the PCC, but you can bring in a specialist and pay them. However, if the PCC fails to find a treasurer at all (or if the treasurer resigns unexpectedly), then the job legally falls to the CWs. When this happened to us – and it started during the interregnum – I did the job for almost eighteen months on my own as I knew that the other CW would not do it, until we had a genuine volunteer come forward. I still do the Gift Aid claims, largely because I wanted to keep the burden for the new volunteer treasurer as light as possible, rather than throw it all at him and run.

Giving

As CW, you should not have much to do with the giving to the church, other than making sure that your own giving is appropriate. However, I think it pays if the CWs have a good working relationship with the treasurer so that they are able to support him when it comes to getting the accounts, budget and unusual spending approved by the PCC. A good understanding of the church finances is most helpful, so that the CW can lead by example in asking good useful questions to the treasurer. Sadly, when the treasurer says, 'Any questions' I have known either complete silence (which tends to suggest that they have no idea about what has just been said) or else there are really poor questions which demonstrate that they have absolutely no idea!

Churches in the past often had large congregations and probably a decent income from endowments and even from the diocese. This gave a good deal of flexibility and stability – if a church wanted to develop a project of any sort, they had lots of scope to pay for it; in those days, the parish share (which is still called "quota" by some) was hardly significant, if it existed at all. Nowadays, the flow of money has definitely reversed, and it is now FROM the parish TO the diocese, and parish share often consumes over 50% of a church's voluntary income, so the question of increasing income is always going to be lurking behind the treasurer's report to the PCC.

I have known a number of ways of increasing the giving by the congregation. This is a task which is often required as individuals will forget to check their standing order annually, and so its value will reduce over time. Other individuals have no real idea of the actual cost of running the church in relation to their own giving and will still think that they are being generous. Hence, some method is needed to make the financial situation clear to the entire regular congregation in order to encourage a realistic level of giving for each individual, whether it is £2 per week or £200 per month. The most successful programme that I have encountered was the TRIO programme, designed originally by the Diocese of Southwark. TRIO is an acronym for "The Responsibility Is Ours", and I have seen an amazing response when it was used at one of the churches I have attended; I do strongly recommend this.

Regular Claims

There are some important financial claims that can be made; I have always found it rewarding to get money back from the government. These claims are:

- Gift Aid
- Gift Aid Small Donations Scheme (GASDS)
- Listed Places of Worship Grant Scheme (re: VAT on major building works)

As before, these do not fall to the CW, but you need to know who does them and that they are done properly and promptly. Gift Aid in particular will form a significant part of the church's income. One of the great legacies of Gordon Brown as Chancellor was the introduction of Gift Aid in place of the old Covenant system. (In fact some might say it was his only great achievement!) I have no idea if it was his idea (probably not) but at least it happened in his time and I am very grateful for it, and every church and charity in the country should be grateful as well.

However, one has to prepare claims for Gift Aid, and a pretty important consideration is to do this regularly. If the annual total being claimed is large, I think it makes sense to make at least four separate claims, and we do ours as follows: Jan 1st – Apr 5th, Apr 6th – Jun 30th, Jul 1st – Sep 30th and Oct 1st – Dec 31st. Even if your claim is small, this routine helps the cash flow. Of course, if your claim is really large then you might even end up doing it monthly. In any event, it is really counter-productive to do it a long time in retrospect; questions will become impossible to answer and you will end up losing money as you will be unsure of the legality of some items. In some dioceses, a scheme is operated where they do make this claim for individual churches. I am unsure how this benefits a church as the main task for each Gift Aid claim is preparing the data, which needs to be done by each church in any case.

GASDS is claimed by the same route but is a totally separate claim. Because there is a maximum amount claimable, you would want to submit this claim as soon as you have reached that maximum in the tax year (i.e., from Apr 6th). I found that one local church with a small income was in the habit of only doing a GASDS claim and not a proper Gift Aid claim. They thought it amounted to the same thing, but I am sure that they were missing out on a significant sum of tax to be claimed, as the maximum individual donation for a GASDS claim is only £20.

Both Gift Aid and GASDS are reclaimed online. It isn't that difficult now that HMRC have introduced web systems that actually do work well.

The Listed Places of Worship Grant Scheme (LPWGS) is the current means by which you can be compensated for the VAT spent on repairs to your church building, subject to certain quite precise conditions. I say "compensated" as legally it is not a claim for the VAT paid out; it is a claim for a grant from the government for a sum of money exactly equal to the VAT you have paid out. This is because EU rules do not allow for easing the VAT rules, and this is a clever way around the rule. The most important condition is that the invoice date is a maximum of one year before the date of the claim, so if you are spending money on making plans for reordering, the odds are that you will not be able to make a claim for some of the preparatory work. At this time, however, it looks as though the writing is on the wall for LPWGS but, hopefully, there will be some other solution.

I once enquired of the commercial contractor responsible for LPWGS why our claim had still not been paid after eight weeks; they told me it would be paid in two weeks time, and the reason for this was that the government had not paid them enough at the right time!

12

The Church Buildings

Love Your Church Building

Old buildings need to be loved and an old church even more so. Of course, brand new ones need to be loved as well, but this love is so important for old buildings. On a newish building, you can have an expectation that many things will continue to work without any maintenance or even thought. Some jobs can be skimped occasionally, and no problem ensues; if there is any problem, the fix is relatively straightforward and probably fairly cheap as there are so many suitable tradespeople available. This simply does not apply to old buildings: if you turn your back on them for a few weeks, or even just days, and neglect some vital maintenance, something bad might happen and the costs can be high.

Church buildings in the UK vary enormously in age and type of construction, from late Saxon churches in flint to very modern buildings in brick, block and cement. It is said that the C of E owns 45% of the Grade I listed buildings in the UK, and these put a huge burden on the church at large. We know that in most cases it is simply neither acceptable nor feasible to close down a church simply because of the high maintenance costs or the need for major repairs costing seven-figure sums. I know of a Baptist church which had a large 19th century building near a town centre; some developers wished to expand the town centre shopping and so the church was moved 100 metres down the road into a brand new purpose-designed building at no cost to the church. Sadly, for most of us, this will never happen; we are where we are, and no one is going to take our ancient churches off our hands and give us a nice new fit-for-purpose building in its place.

Sadly, many older church buildings have suffered from poor maintenance or simply a lack of love. When this happens even just for a few years, it can be very difficult to return the building to a fit state where it "only" requires regular maintenance. If you don't sort out problems at the first sign of trouble (either yourself or by having someone you can call on to do it) then you can incur a huge cost in due course. For instance, dampness in a wall may cause the lime plaster to "pop" – it comes away from the wall and sounds hollow when you tap it with your knuckles, before eventually gently falling off. The only solution then is to strip it off entirely and replaster at considerable expense (and much mess). One church I know had a perennially freezing vestry which, when I investigated, was caused by the ground outside being higher than the floor inside; sadly, the plaster had popped long ago. The old proverb "a stitch in time saves nine" is even more true for old buildings – a repair in time probably saves 999, in financial terms.

So, I encourage you to love your church building. If it is at all old, it will have lots of history, some of it hidden, waiting to be uncovered, so get to know the whole building. There are nooks and crannies all over the place – it took me years at Clamcester to discover that there was a whole room in the tower above the bell-ringers' room, and even longer to get access to the belfry itself. At every church, this has seemed to be the preserve of the tower captain, but during the latest quinquennial the architect wanted to get inside. I said that I didn't have a key and the architect suggested looking in the ringing room – and there it was, hanging on the wall! Mind you, even then I would not have gone in if the bells had been "up" – that's very dangerous.

Even a Victorian church is likely to have some quirks, with memorials of note. If you have an interest in history, or know someone in the local history society, then develop that interest and look at the church with a different eye. You might have the opportunity on many occasions to welcome visitors to the church, and you might even give guided tours at some time. Putting these details on your church website may also help to produce some surprising discoveries.

Here are some of the interesting things that I have found or experienced due to my interest in the quirks of the church and my willingness to show people around:

1. At Bogthornly, the east window had been removed in World War II for safe keeping. When it was restored in the early fifties, some panels from the bottom (showing a pair of supporting pillars) were refitted near the top – by mistake or intention?
2. At the same church, a memorial had a really sweet inscription by a husband to his wife who died aged

twenty-one, and there was an unfixed memorial in the gallery to the husband, who for a short time in the 19th century had been a Member of Parliament. I had an idea of refixing that one beneath the wife's memorial where it clearly belonged, but one day I had an email from someone who had seen these details on the church website. She told me that she was writing a book about him – he was an absolute rogue who stole the investors' money from his savings bank and, in her view, he had probably killed his young wife! I'm afraid that I rapidly dropped the idea of refixing his memorial.

3. I was showing a group of visitors the east window at Bogthornly and remarked that I was puzzled about the detail of the bearded gentleman who looked a bit out of place because of the intricate detail on his face; one of the visitors suggested that he was probably my distant predecessor as CW from the time when the window was fitted, as this was a known practice.

4. At Clamcester, there are some wonderful handmade forged hinges on the door of the bell-ringers' chamber in the tower, sadly rarely seen by visitors and probably unappreciated by the bell-ringers. These hinges probably date from when the tower was made in the 15th century, although I reckon the door has been replaced several times in that time.

5. Also at Clamcester, some of the stones on the parapet of the porch were found to have been previously used when we rebuilt the parapet, and we found carved graffiti in the stone in several places on the tower.

6. I once had some visitors from France who contacted me by email. They wished to visit and I had no idea of precisely why they had come; the Frenchman spoke English which was better than my French, but

my French was better than his wife's English, so we
managed (just). Whilst showing them round, I showed
them a bell dated from 1219, which was displayed in the
church, and read out the details on a notice underneath.
As I did so, I realised that the surname on the notice was
also their surname. This bell was what they had come to
see, having traced their lineage back almost 800 years!

7. I've already mentioned having a visit from a couple
from Australia. He had been in the Royal Australian
Air Force in the war and they had married in 1945
in the church where we stood. To celebrate their
diamond wedding anniversary, this was their first visit
back to the UK since then. It is an honour to meet
people like that.

8. Then there are the names written on the wall of the
tower spiral stairway of bell-ringers from years ago,
or the names carved on the wooden wall behind the
organ by the bored boys whose job it was to pump
the organ during services, or the 18th century brass
chandelier engraved with the misspelt name of the
donor, or the error in a stained glass window where
the captions for the panels are under the wrong panel.
Examples abound, if you keep your eyes open.

I have two favourite "discoveries" in churches. One was
a particular stained glass window – you might ask, how
can you discover a stained glass window? Well, it lacked
natural light, being in the north aisle, and there was a very
large spherical laurel tree outside which blocked what
light there was. I wanted to chop it down entirely, but
eventually the PCC agreed to a "severe prune". The 25-
foot high tree was reduced to a set of ten stems about
eight feet high, which look very bare but will surely
regrow; the real benefit was inside where the window

was now displayed in all its glory. Even with just the northern light behind it, we could now see the real beauty of this creation, with multiple shades of red, green, blue and brown, depicting two scenes of the life of St Peter. Apparently it had been hidden in full view for over thirty years. The added maintenance task of regular trimming is a small price to pay for such a treasure.

The other discovery was getting to the top of the tower at Bogthornly. The squat tower was square with a domed roof with an apparently inaccessible cupola on top; inside, the tower was octagonal with a vaulted ceiling. I noticed that there appeared to be the makings of a fixed ladder in one of the corners created between the square and the octagon. Sure enough, climbing the ladder with some care, I found myself between the vaulted ceiling and the roof, and there was a trapdoor! Opening this, I was able to climb into the cupola and survey the elevated view across the rooftops. Darren, the verger's helper, followed me up and sat down beside me. 'I've been here for twenty years and I did not know this existed!' he said. Feeling pleased with myself, I sent an email to the church architect, telling him about my discovery. His reply was deflating: 'Didn't you know about that? I was up there on the last Quinquennial!'

Hopefully, you understand what I mean by "loving your church building". It has history, and that history comes to life as you find out more about it and share it with others – you can learn from them just as they can learn from you, and you feel the richer for it. As you care for it, you will see its condition improve little by little; your aim as CW should be to pass on to your successor, when you finish your term, a church building which is measurably better than the one you took over.

The Church Architect

Every church must have an appointed church architect. He is not just any architect; he must have a recognised qualification regarding church buildings and also has to be on the diocesan list of approved architects. The appointed architect is an individual, not a company or partnership, even if he works for one or owns it. He is engaged by the church, and the church should put a lot of effort into finding the right one. If your church does not have the right one for any reason, then the PCC should consider terminating the relationship and finding a new one. The DAC will help you in this, by recommending people from their list who they think are suitable for the peculiarities of your building.

Strangely, I have known of some architects who had the wrong view about this relationship; they seemed to think that they were the final arbiter in all matters relating to the church building, and the CWs and PCCs seemed to regard them with awe as some sort of higher being. This is so wrong! The architect is engaged by the PCC and has to recommend matters to the PCC; he has no right to insist on anything – if he thinks he has then make it clear to him that he doesn't. Hopefully, if he doesn't agree, then he will realise that his option is to move on and let someone else work for you.

I know of one CW who bitterly regretted losing an argument with the architect; a new external door required protective treatment and the PCC wanted to use a solvent-based material to stain and protect the door, whilst the architect said the door should be varnished. Sadly, somehow the architect won; five years later, the PCC had to pay for the door to be stripped of the peeling varnish and then be stained, just as the CW had desired in the first place.

Of course, if the CWs and no one else on the PCC have no idea about such matters, then you really will have to do precisely what the architect recommends. Even then, though, you should be asking intelligently for justification of recommendations and making sure that you are not being blindly forced down a narrow road of his choosing. It is the church that is paying for the works, and exercising the charitable responsibilities of the PCC means a lot more is involved than a simple blind acceptance. You need to be absolutely sure of your architect if you are doing a major reordering project without a competent person on your side who is independent and will advise the PCC on the suitability (or otherwise) of the architect's recommendations.

I got off to an interesting start with an architect once, when I was new to a church: some drawings for our project were spread out on the meeting table for us to peruse. You can often see people's eyes glaze over at such a moment but, as an engineer, I am not fazed by such drawings. Almost at once I said, 'This limecrete floor is almost exactly the same design as the one in my kitchen.' The architect replied, 'Who laid that for you?' and was clearly a bit surprised when I said, 'I did it myself!' That brief exchange established my technical credibility, and since that moment we got on very well.

Let me give you a few examples of the sort of pitfalls that are likely to occur:

1. You want to install a new lighting system in your church. The architect should give you a good number of options of the style of lighting, not just two or three; this is a fundamental choice that you and your congregation will live with for years, so it has to be a well-informed choice, not an either/or.

2. In the same way, you will need some controls on your lighting, and you are told how fantastic a particular system is, albeit expensive. The crucial questions are: who does have control and how will you change the settings on this system? Be aware that the answer may be that you have to engage the original contractor at great expense each time to do even the smallest change; I suggest that this is a situation in which you do not want to be.

3. You also need to think about the running costs of the system. How big will the electricity bills be? What are the ongoing maintenance costs, such as replacement bulbs? How easy is it to replace light bulbs? One church I know had a new system with halogen bulbs installed at a time when the rest of the world was starting to fit LEDs, which are far more efficient in terms of electricity consumption; the electricity bills are quite high. Of course, the available LED bulbs require different fittings, so changing about eighty fittings now would be extremely expensive.

4. Don't be afraid to question the architect – it is you who will pay for and live with the decisions, not him, so if something is not clear to you then you must ask for clarification. Don't forget that you (the church) are the customer, and the PCC are responsible in law for spending the charity's money wisely.

5. He should specify a retention of money in your contract, often 2½% or even 5% retained for a year.

This is to allow for the subsequent discovery of issues which may become apparent in that time and so is the opportunity for you to insist on value for money; if you find things wrong in the first twelve months, you can insist on them being fixed at no cost before the retention is released – it's your church's money, not the architect's! For the project done at Clamcester before I arrived, there was no retention; several minor issues went unnoticed and uncorrected, such as a single light having a different shade of white to all the others – how did the architect not spot that?

6. The architect should check the quality of the work, but don't be afraid to check the obvious things yourself. The wrong things might be as simple as that incorrect light bulb (above) or a switch which works in the opposite sense to all the others. More difficult to fix, there might be an inoperative light fitting (a failure of both the contractor's and the architect's inspections) or a light fitting omitted entirely (possibly a misunderstanding by the architect or contractor).

7. You may need to remind the architect that the final decision will always be made by the church, not by him. I have found that, in general, architects (and not just church architects) are very good at suggesting ways of spending money which isn't theirs. Of course, as a rule, no church is awash with money (if yours is, please tell me), so that decision must include consideration of the ongoing costs (such as utility bills or routine maintenance) as well as the initial capital costs. Being tied in to a specific contractor for maintenance and/or change is a recipe for future expense; if the contractor/supplier is seeing the church as part of their future income stream, then I suggest that they may be the wrong contractor. You need to choose systems that are

maintainable by any qualified person, not just by the one specialist supplier.

The architect of course has to be paid. For the Quinquennial Inspection, a fixed rate should be agreed in advance, but other work is probably done at an hourly rate which should be agreed at the outset – the standard RIBA rate is a good figure to use in a letter of engagement. However, if you have a contract for a major project, the architect will probably be paid a percentage of the total contract cost (excluding VAT), so don't be surprised by an increase in the fees if you expand the contract.

Insurance

Your church must be insured. This is pretty obvious and should already be the case, but I do suggest that you check the policy and the exclusions as soon as you take over as CW. I asked to see the policy before I became CW at Bogthornly, but the vicar, the existing CWs and the treasurer could not produce it! It was found eventually, but by then I had already contacted the insurers who confirmed that we were indeed insured. That sort of omission would keep me awake at night.

Then you must check that the insurance is adequate for your needs, and someone should be the nominated contact for the insurers. The details of the insurance policy might be quite different from your house or car insurance, so the CWs need to be aware of these details. You might have someone else who looks after it, possibly the treasurer, but his main interest might be to reduce the cost, whereas the CW's concern is for the building itself. Naturally, insurance claims will come out of the blue – a fire, a theft of roof lead, or a vandalised stained glass window, for instance. In such cases, you need to hope that there are no problems with your insurance. Check the policy carefully now (not after the event!), looking in particular at any exclusions with particular reference to theft (e.g., of lead) and damage.

The major insurer of Anglican churches is Ecclesiastical Insurance, and they have been the insurer of all the C of E churches at which I have held office. They employ surveyors who visit insured churches on a regular but infrequent basis, to check that the insurance fits the needs of the church. If you have not been visited in the last eight or ten years, I suggest that you ask your insurer when the next visit is likely. At Clamcester, it turned out that the last visit had been seventeen years previously, and a surveyor duly arrived one day. I queried whether the insurance was index-linked – it was, but the insured value had to be revised as the index-linking had varied over that long period of time. When there had been a fire at Bogthornly, the loss adjuster's first statement to the church was that we were underinsured due to lack of index-linking. Happily the previously mentioned brigadier (who was the vice-chair of the PCC) knew his stuff and produced a letter where he had requested that the policy be index-linked – the fact that they had not done this was irrelevant and so they duly paid out in full.

I had a discussion with the surveyor about the level of the insurance, which was set at 75% rather than the expected 100%. I was concerned about this, as if your house insurance is too low, all claims will be factored (i.e., reduced proportionately). The surveyor told me that the way they work is different: they start with an insured value, and 100% insurance gives cover for a complete rebuild of the church. However, from their experience, they know that if a limestone church has a fire, there will almost certainly be a shell of structure left afterwards, and so 75% cover will be adequate to rebuild. If a church is not listed and is potentially redundant, then if there is a catastrophic fire, it won't be rebuilt, and just 25% insurance will be sufficient to demolish what is left and clear the site. Make sure that your church insurance is appropriate.

At Clamcester, we had an issue with the damage to a stained glass window when we found that the insurance policy had an exclusion saying that such windows were only covered if protected by a stainless steel mesh. Sadly, the damaged one was the only one protected by a copper mesh – the other nine were all stainless steel. This one was quite high up and we simply had never noticed or even considered that the blackish mesh might not be steel. When I pointed out to the loss adjuster that an insurance surveyor had been to the church four years previously and had not noticed it either, Ecclesiastical were very good and agreed that he should have commented on it (and then we would have fixed it), so they paid for the whole job – and the new mesh was of course stainless steel. It was only at the subsequent quinquennial that I saw the tell-tale verdigris below the window which should have been spotted by both the surveyor and me years earlier.

The Quinquennial Inspection

One of the questions asked at the Archdeacon's inspection is the date of the last Quinquennial Inspection (QI), which is a detailed check of the church building, performed by the church architect. I'd like to assume that every church does have these inspections, even if that is perhaps sometimes at more than five-year intervals! The resulting Quinquennial Inspection Report (QIR) contains recommendations for items of work, some of which should be done immediately and some others urgently.

The CWs need to be aware of the recommendations of the QIR. These include the immediate ones which may be cheap and simple and can be done at once, such as clearing rubbish or drains; however, you might also have something really expensive that needs to be done at once if you have let things slide. Then there are the urgent ones which need addressing in the next year – these can be large projects which might require careful planning with a high cost, and hopefully you are already aware of the need and are developing a plan. Finally there are the less urgent ones; these might be strategic issues, routine repairs or less important details which are for the longer term future. These should nevertheless be addressed in some way; otherwise one day they will become urgent.

Like many other things, the QIR can get glossed over. They should have increased in detail in recent years – only twenty years ago, ours at Clamcester were just three or four pages long, written in the most general terms and really quite useless. The ones we now get (from a different architect) are fifty or sixty pages, which if anything is almost too detailed but, if you are going to do conservation and renovation works on the church, this is to be preferred to brevity.

Together, the QIR and the Archdeacon's inspection will probably give the CWs plenty to do, in addition to the normal requirements of services, meetings and maintenance.

There will be many other calls on your time, which you must prioritise without forgetting that these fundamentals will not go away; they require continuous attention, or things might get worse. For old buildings, "getting worse" tends to mean that a delay in fixing something will cause the final cost to be significantly greater. The classic example of this is when a hopper at the top of a downpipe gets blocked. If someone gets up there (even in the rain) and clears it as soon as it is discovered, all will probably be well. However, if it is ignored and forgotten for months or even a year or two, the result might be that the damp wall now needs expensive replastering. In my time as CW, I have been up on a safe church roof (with a parapet) in pouring rain at least four times, with an umbrella in one hand and a decent stick in the other, clearing a hopper with a blockage caused by sticks from nesting birds which had become evident when water poured down the wall inside. Equally, leaves and moss can easily block gutters and hoppers, so you need to check frequently if any of these apply to your church. This sort of thing will form the basis of your inspection schedule.

I have seen how easy it is for CWs to ignore the minor tasks, such as replacement of broken leaded lights. When you need to get someone in because there's a new break in one of those diamond-shaped pieces in leaded windows, check and see just how many more similar repairs are outstanding (now you know why the church was so cold and the heating bill so high). Or perhaps it is small faults like electrical sockets not working, or light bulbs broken, or bits of pew which are loose, or loose floor tiles… the list could be long. In four weeks over last Christmas, I fixed a broken kitchen unit, a broken table, a new loo seat and the wiring for the light for the nativity display.

I encourage you to not let that sort of thing get out of hand; honestly, if you sort out these small things on a regular basis, one day you will get to the end of the list. The trick is to identify and tackle the urgent tasks whilst still keeping all the boring ones ticking over – ideally, get some small ones done at the same time as getting a larger job done by the same contractor. This requires a balance between ignoring all the maintenance and routine tasks just because they are by nature routine and boring, and letting your time get filled by them to the detriment of the bigger picture.

The last QI at Clamcester was done just before I ended my six years as CW, so I had been CW for the complete period covered. I was pretty happy with the pretty impressive list in the QIR of work done during the quinquennium, and very pleased with the summary: *The vicar, CWs and others should be commended for hard work since the last QI* and *It is worth noting the great achievements of the last five years*. This is well-deserved praise for the team who have worked so hard with me, and it doesn't get much better than that!

Faculties

"Faculty". The very word can strike gloom or even terror into the heart of many a CW. Sadly, the faculty is something that we cannot do without. There was a time when the incumbent of a parish had all sorts of rights and there was literally no one to whom he (and it was a "he" then) was answerable. The faculty system was devised to bring them under some sort of control, at least as far as buildings go. However, like Topsy, the system grew and the form to petition (not "ask" or "apply") for a faculty grew in complexity and frustration.

Now, the C of E usually moves exceedingly slowly, but recently something happened quickly in regard to faculties. There is now an online system for faculty petitions which is a vast improvement on the old system of filling in a huge form each time and sending it off with a mass of attached documents in a heavy envelope. I am told that this new system was very cheap and I have found that, perhaps surprisingly, it works. (If the C of E can do this cheaply, why can't my bank, with all their millions?) The online system mimics the old process and allows each Diocesan Advisory Committee (DAC) to control the process in their own way, so don't expect it to work in exactly the same way if you move to a new diocese. However, be clear that the DAC simply makes recommendations to the Chancellor about your petition – even if they disagree, you can still send it to the Chancellor for him to decide. One of the annoying items is that the relevant "heritage bodies" also need to be consulted but, again, their dissent does not necessarily stop the Chancellor approving your petition. We once had a difficulty in actually getting a comment from them at all, even to say "no objection".

The DAC Secretary is your friend as far as faculties go. You should go to her for advice as soon as you think you want to petition for a faculty. Even with the new system, you still need lots of information, you have to answer lots of questions and you might just find it a bit irritating, as the online form still has exactly the same questions as the old paper form. These questions say things like *Please answer this section in every case… If required, has outline or full planning permission or advertisement consent been granted? Yes/No.* So if this isn't required, do you answer *No*, or do you leave it blank? Why can't they have a *Not Applicable* option? I'm told that the reason why this has not changed is that it would require General Synod to approve it – I guess they have better things to do with their time.

Apart from the ease of online application, they have also achieved the introduction of a new level of approval. In earlier times, there existed a thing called the "de minimis" list. This was a list of the things that you could do without a faculty, and if it wasn't on the list then you had to go down the full faculty route. I don't doubt that many people stretched their interpretation of it well beyond the intended scope in order to avoid using the faculty petition form! The "de minimis" list is now called "List A" and functions in the same way. The recent innovation was the introduction of "List B" which is a list of the things that the Archdeacon can approve as a faculty, hopefully saving both you and the Chancellor of the diocese much work in processing a full faculty. You still raise the petition online, but when you go down the List B route, there is much less information required and, with luck, the Archdeacon will approve it in a matter of a couple of weeks or so (provided you have provided the correct information and anticipated the possible questions).

All this information on the faculty process should be readily available from the DAC, probably via the diocesan website. If you are in an old church, I would expect that in three to five years in the job, you should need to do several faculties – if you don't, you have either had an amazing predecessor who got the place really in order, or else you haven't read your last Quinquennial Report!

People worry about planning permission: this is normally only required for works that affect the exterior of a church, but it seems to help your petition if you can get an email from the appropriate council saying that planning permission is not required. You should also be aware that work in the churchyard is controlled by faculty as well, even if it is maintained by the local council – see the later chapter on Churchyards.

When a faculty is granted, you will receive a copy (or copies) from the registrar's office; one of these will probably be the official copy with an embossed stamp or some other legal device. Do make sure to keep this one safely, and take copies as required – one for the church architect, one for the contractor and another for your own files.

I cannot stress too highly the importance of adhering to the correct faculty process. The faculty, once granted, is your legal approval to do the work that is specified, in the manner specified. If you stray from the drawings that have been approved as part of the faculty process, then you are straying into dubious legal territory. Even using (say) a different colour of paint may cause problems, and using a different type of paint probably will. Similarly, with regard to Lists A and B, I do not recommend stretching the point. If such point stretching is possible, it should be done with the agreement (possibly a blind eye) of the DAC and/or the Archdeacon. You can land yourself in all sorts of legal hot water if you ignore the drawings or stretch the point and get found out; it can get embarrassing and even personally expensive. Occasionally, *Church Times* has an article about some legal problem which I always find of interest; there have been a couple where a vicar and the CWs were criticised heavily (and penalised financially) by a Consistory Court because of their failure to follow the basic rules for faculties. You have been warned!

13

Principles Of Old Buildings

Most churches are old. If you are fortunate, yours is relatively new and built using modern materials, but most old buildings are different. Why?

The key word is "lime". Old buildings were built using lime, not cement. Many Roman structures built with lime mortar still survive, after almost 2,000 years, but cement was invented in the 19th century and only became really widespread in the Second World War.

If you take one thing away from this book, it is that *you should not use modern materials (which are all based on cement) or modern techniques (like a chemical damp proof course) on an old building*. Too many buildings have been effectively ruined by such actions, sadly as a result of the ignorance of architects and contractors and approved by a PCC who accepted their advice.

If you would take a second fact away from this book, it is the advice from a young architect to a one-day course I attended some years back, in company with a dozen or so other CWs. She said:

- 'If you look after the water which falls on the church's roof,
- then flows into the gutters,
- into the hoppers,
- down the drainpipes,
- into the drains
- and away from the building,
- then you have done four-fifths of the job and the church will not fall down on your watch.'

Read that statement again – read it until you understand and accept it. Then read on and I'll tell you why these two statements are so fundamental to the long-term integrity of your old church.

Firstly, lime. The reason for the longevity of Roman buildings is that they were made using lime mortar. Lime is calcium hydroxide (CaOH) and it makes a wonderful mortar. When exposed to the air, it very slowly attracts carbon dioxide (CO_2) from the atmosphere. The result is that water (H_2O) is given off and the lime becomes calcium carbonate ($CaCO_3$) which is basically limestone, i.e., solid rock. (You can relax now; that's the end of the technical chemical explanations.) Because this action takes place over decades, the lime mortar is not fully set until the transformation is complete, so the mortar is flexible and does not crack easily. Lime mortar is porous (the water has to get out) even when it is fully set, because after all limestone itself is porous.

Conversely, cement mortar is rigid so a small shock can break its join with another material, and it is thus permanently weakened. Cement mortar is about 3,000 times less porous than lime, which makes it virtually impervious, and it does not expand and contract with temperature. Since limestone does expand and contract with temperature, where cement has been used on limestone, the join between the two is weakened by each daily rise and fall in temperature as the lime expands and the cement doesn't. If someone has touched up parts of your limestone church with cement, you will see that where it is thin then a crack can form and it easily breaks away, even if dry.

Now, in a wall, the mortar between stones or bricks is designed to be the means by which any water in that wall can escape by preferential evaporation (and water will get into the wall as limestone is porous, remember?). This is usually referred to as "breathability". If you use cement mortar in the wall or even just repoint on lime mortar with cement mortar, the wall can no longer breathe, that moisture cannot escape and so it can only go to one place – into the stone itself. If those bricks or stones are damp, when winter comes, the water freezes and expands, and the surface of the stone or brick is lost as the ice particles force the surface of the limestone or brick apart. Repeat this process over many times in many winters and the surface of the wall has now retreated into the wall, leaving the cement pointing standing proud. This can, sadly, be seen on very many old buildings, including listed ones, and it makes me weep.

Now, do you want that to happen to your 900-year-old Grade I listed church? Just ask yourself why it survived the first 800 years – because no one used cement on it!

In respect of floors, a similar issue arises. A limecrete floor is made using lime mortar, not cement (which would make it "concrete") and the result is breathable, thus any dampness underneath can escape by evaporation through the floor. In a concrete floor, the water cannot escape and eventually it is liable to reach the walls where it rises a bit and causes permanent dampness in the walls, which makes lime plaster fall off. In such a case, please do not believe people who say that "a bit of thistle plaster will fix that", because it doesn't. It might be cheaper, but all that happens is that the modern pink plaster has a permanent cold feeling and the dampness goes even further up the wall.

Secondly, water. What lime does not like is to be damp for any length of time. If you have a leaking gutter or blocked hopper and do not fix it, the wall underneath will be damp. It will not dry out as, once really wet, drying a thick limestone wall can take a year or two, and it will rain again before then! Hence, the mortar in the wall, and any lime plaster on the inside, will be continually damp and gently perish over a period. First, the internal plaster becomes detached (or "popped"), and then the mortar eventually turns to damp sand. Such issues will cost a huge sum to fix, compared to the relatively small cost of fixing the gutter or hopper or downpipe in the first place. This is why it is so important to check your rainwater goods during a good rainstorm, carrying a large umbrella and a pair of binoculars; at those times you can see exactly where water flows and note any places where leaves or birds have blocked a hopper, downpipe or drain, or where there are any leaks from cracked pipes, etc.

In the same way, people like to make paths look neat and lay a concrete (i.e., cement-based) path right up to a wall. The result is that every time it rains, the splashback from the rainfall makes the bottom 6" – 12"damp, which eventually penetrates through to the internal wall. In due course, the mortar gives up and you are left with a wall which has holes in the pointing. Then someone comes along with some cement and makes it all look good, but in a year or two there is still dampness showing on the wall inside.

A modern "solution" is to apply a chemical damp proof course (DPC) to a limestone wall. At best, this is simply a waste of money; and at worst, it will do irreparable damage to the wall. The chemicals just do not work on lime in the same way that they do on cement. The trouble is that some salesman will come along pretending to be a specialist with years of training, and say that his little instrument shows that you have dampness and the only solution is to apply a chemical DPC. Please do not believe him – he is a salesman who knows nothing about old buildings and is just trying to make a living. Feel sorry for him by all means, but do not fall for his pitch.

Another cause of dampness in walls is common to many churches: higher ground outside will ensure that a wall is permanently damp. Of course, many churches suffer from this – how many churches do you know where you step up into the church? More often you step down, thanks to ever-rising churchyard levels and a few Tractarian principles from the Victorians, who seemed to consider it a good idea to lower the nave floor. If your church suffers from damp in walls, there is no point in replastering until you have taken steps to dry out the wall, probably with a French drain (and definitely not with a waterproof membrane or chemical DPC). If you replaster too soon, it will fall off as it just won't set and adhere properly to the wall. Equally, there is no point in turning up the heating to combat dampness – it will not dry out the wall as there is a continual supply of dampness from the outside, so all you do is waste energy and money by continually trying to convert that never-ending dampness into water vapour.

NB A "French drain" is nothing to do with the country across the Channel, but rather it was designed by someone called Henry French, who was American. It's a very useful method and relatively simple way of making the walls of your church drier. You'll find details online quite easily.

The other cause of dampness is vegetation, often ivy. People might think it looks nice, but seriously, anything which grows up the walls of the church (and I do mean inside as well as outside!) is not good for it. Ivy in particular is really quite nasty, partly because it grows so quickly – before you know it, it's out of reach, blocking gutters and even penetrating through walls. A tree growing close to the wall will restrict the evaporation of any water in the wall and so may promote dampness, quite apart from depositing leaves in gutters. Moss is also bad – it retains a lot of water and thus ensures that the wall is always damp. If you remove a bit of moss from a limestone wall, you will often find that it feels a bit sandy – that is indeed sand which has come from the deterioration of the limestone wall!

Your church may have suspended wooden floors – the Victorians liked them a lot, it seems. The issue with these floors is that they are so often damp. This is because the ground underneath them (usually a foot or so under the floorboards) is basically just bare ground and so is also damp. Over the years, the dampness has increased and never decreased, and so the whole area is an ideal place for damp rot to flourish. The thing is, you see, that the Victorians did not really understand the need for ventilation. They sometimes made provision for a few very small vents and thought that was adequate. It isn't. If they had understood more and done that job better with many much larger vents, it would now be far harder to get rid of the pews and the pew platforms as they would still be in good condition. As it is, most of these pews and floors really need replacement; and by fitting something different, we can also sort out those annoying little steps that appear everywhere in a Victorian church, causing issues for the less able. By the way, I should mention here that woodworm (actually a beetle) cannot survive in dry conditions, so if your church is watertight and heated, you have probably eliminated all woodworm except under the damp suspended floor. If in doubt, look for the loose wood dust ("frass") which is usually evidence of recent activity.

Before I arrived at Clamcester, a reordering project had been carried out, and in that time the church architect had forwarded an unsolicited proposal from the main contractor to do a chemical DPC on this old limestone church. Fortunately, they had rejected this proposal but, if I had been present, I would have said that the only valid reply was to fire the architect (who was properly authorised to be a church architect but clearly knew less than me about such matters).

Too many architects and building contractors will say disparaging things like 'You don't believe all that stuff, do you?' and 'We'll add a bit of lime to the mix. That'll make it all right'. These points of view seem to be held by about 90% of such professional people in my experience, and they are completely wrong. (Adding hydrated lime to a mix makes it easier to mix and work, but does absolutely nothing to help breathability.) You might have to argue with them, and they might even try to say "yes" but still do it their way when you are not looking; don't forget you are the customer and the job is being done for a much longer timescale than they normally consider. Their view is the next ten or twenty years; churches need the longest lasting repair possible – say 100 or 200 years – that is why they have survived so long. Make sure that the use of lime putty is specified in the contract, and check that they are using it.

At this stage, I will mention that in restoring our 150-year-old house, I used only the traditional materials and techniques, and we removed over 130 tonnes (net) of material from the site, most of it earth from along two sides where the ground level was too high and so encouraged dampness. The result is a house which now is dry and warm. Once, we were talking about the proposed new limecrete floor in part of the church, and people were arguing about sealing the floor. I sat on my hands with my tongue between my teeth for about ten minutes, and then finally I said: 'We are not sealing the floor as it has to breathe. I do know what I'm talking about – I have a house across the road that proves it.' End of discussion. When I mentioned this to the DAC secretary and asked why this wasn't spelt out in the faculty, she said, 'I thought it was obvious'!

Finally, on old buildings, another important principle is: *always address the cause of a problem, not the symptom*. The modern builder's view may well be that you just cover it up and it will go away for five or ten years. However, conversely, you are conserving the church for posterity, not for just your brief tenancy, so you must always take the long-term view, even if it is more expensive (as it will be). If you address just the symptom, the problem will always recur, possibly even whilst you are still in the post, and so you would actually be wasting the money rather than saving it.

To summarise: don't use modern materials on old buildings, and look after the water!

14

Reordering And
Major Repairs

In my six years as CW at Clamcester, we have completed
four major reordering or repair projects (including one
during our interregnum), and these followed on from
another such project a year before I arrived – total
expenditure (including VAT) was about £1.2m in eight
years. One reason for this is that we have been blessed
at Clamcester with having a very experienced church
project fundraiser living in the parish. Without her, I am
sure that we would not have achieved even half of these
projects. We also have a strong team which includes people
with experience of tenders, contracts and understanding
technical drawings, as well as knowledge of the techniques
of working on old buildings. In doing these projects, we
have all learned a lot (such as how to navigate through
the application process for the Heritage Lottery Fund, and
where on the church you might find a merlon), and we
have worked hard together; make no mistake, these projects
are hard work. Together we have made a pretty good team,
and we have the results to prove it.

Sadly, you will probably not be so fortunate in terms of the personnel available, but even if you can get one project off the ground then you will be making an impact. The trick here is to divide the work into achievable projects without them getting too small; unless you have a very strong and experienced team, a really large project will be in the preparation stage for a decade and is likely to founder eventually without any significant achievement. You will need lots of money; this can come from fundraising, gifts, legacies or grants. Naturally, one cannot plan for legacies, but you can sow the seeds for the future by producing and publicising a legacy leaflet. I was quite disappointed at one church when a wealthy church member died and left absolutely nothing to the church, although her adult family all shared at least the £1m value of her large, old house. Clearly, we had failed somewhere.

The other three sources (fundraising, gifts and grants) are all, frankly, hard work. Fundraising large sums requires some serious hard work and planning, but even then you might end up with "only" a few thousand pounds where you hoped for tens of thousands. Gifts depend very largely on the nature of your congregation – again, it would be a wealthy and generous congregation who would give a serious sum of money in a short time. That leaves grants, which can also be hard work. The application forms for Lottery funds are enough to put off even hardened fundraisers, but tackling them might be your best bet for decent sums; however, you might well need to engage a professional fundraiser. You might have some success with raising loans from the congregation or interested local parties, but don't forget that these don't really count as fundraising as they will need to be repaid at some time – they only really help the cash flow.

The obvious grant-making body to approach is the Heritage Lottery Fund. Their process is long and complex, which is hardly surprising when you are asking for six-figure sums. Our first application was turned down, but we were encouraged to apply again and we were successful twice. Developing a healthy relationship with them was a major part of this success as grant-making bodies need to have the confidence that you know what you are doing and that they can trust you.

However, if you are planning on reordering, don't start with fundraising: before you do that, you need to think about what you actually want to do in your church. What is your mission? What sort of activities? So what do these things tell you about the work you need to do in the church? There are only a few projects which fit in the "no-brainer" category here – possibly things like disabled access and a hearing aid loop – but everything else is totally dependent on what you want to do with the reordered church. There is no point in saying 'let's get rid of the pews' without knowing precisely how this will benefit your mission. So identify that mission first, and then see how you could adapt the church to meet that identified need, not the other way round. Even the exact form of the disabled access and the positioning of the hearing aid loop will depend, to some extent, on what you are planning to do with it.

Major repairs are probably easier to identify. These will almost certainly have been mentioned in the QIR, and those with a high priority obviously need the first attention. It is probably fair to say that a major issue like a roof liable to collapse will certainly hinder your mission! If your church is listed and is also on the Historic England Register of

Churches At Risk, then your chances of obtaining grants will be improved. When the church at Clamcester was placed on that register, they apologised and said that it was no reflection on us, but rather it was intended to help us with raising finance – and I believe it did. However, we now expect it to be removed from that register as the building itself is in a much improved condition.

Most of our projects have been related to the condition of the building; don't fall into the trap of rejecting a project because you feel that it would be too difficult or too expensive. You never know until you actually ask people to give a tender whether the cost will be as budgeted – many jobs that you or I would think are really difficult are the bread and butter of good contractors, and thus cheaper than you might think. I have been amazed at the skill of some of our contractors when they have removed parts of a hood moulding or 17 metres of carved stone wall or large stones that seem to be major structural items. Days later, these parts are replaced with newly cut and carved stone, and the cost was not as much as I feared. The sign of skill is not just being able to do a difficult job but also the speed at which a high-quality job is done. As a philosophical bricklayer once told me, 'Anyone can lay bricks, but not everyone can do it fast enough to make money!'

Apart from the obvious task of drawing up the plans, the architect will assist in the preparation of tenders, the identification of potential contractors and the supervision and acceptance of the work. There will be staged payments as the work progresses, based on the architect and contractor agreeing the value of the work done so far. Prompt payment is always a good idea; unless you have a genuine query with the invoice, there is no point in delaying payment, and it makes your contractor happy to work with you again.

Apart from the architect, another vital team member on a major project is a quantity surveyor; he has a number of important functions relating to the projected cost of proposals from the architect and also may be asked to assess tenders. In particular, the apparently cheapest tender is actually not always the cheapest in the end. Beware of any "Provisional Sums" in a tender as that means that the potential contractor is not able or willing to put a cost to those particular items; the unknown actual sum, whatever it is, will be payable by the customer, not the contractor. Our architect was a bit worried about the appointment of the quantity surveyor until he realised that it meant that he did not have to carry the burden on his own, as someone else was being paid to check his work and share the responsibility.

Nowadays, the grant-making bodies tend to ask for evidence of how your project will show improved community engagement – they don't want to give money to your church just to improve the condition of a monument to the past; they want to see more people using your church in future as a result of their generosity. The understanding now is that a building will survive better if it is used more. Naturally, this means that introducing toilet facilities and disabled access are much easier to justify than some all-embracing proposal that the church will be used for a multitude of poorly defined community projects which are all at the embryonic stage. You may well find that some less important jobs can be usefully done at the same time as a high-priority task. This applies especially if you are using scaffolding – do everything you can with it whilst it's up, especially if it's around the church tower. A person at the Heritage Lottery Fund once told me that they 'would only pay once for scaffolding round a church tower.' Doing as much as possible as one project will work out cheaper than having two or three smaller projects at different times – the cost of both your architect and contractor will reduce due to the economy of scale, and contractors tend to have a fixed sum for overheads, regardless of whether the job lasts three weeks or three months. So, do your research and consider your options carefully – then go for it!

15

Maintenance Work

Most churches are old buildings, and maintenance of an old building is not optional. Maintenance must be done with an appropriate regularity, and to an appropriate depth. I have already mentioned my version of the old saying that "A stitch in time saves nine" – for an old building in terms of cost, it should read: "A stitch in time saves 999". This is because if, for example, you do not ensure the hopper and gutters are clear, rainwater will run down and into the walls and eventually the lime plaster will fall off the wall. The financial cost of replacing this is huge, quite apart from the mess and disruption caused.

There is much guidance available online, and in particular the C of E has a website called *Churchcare* (http://www. churchcare.co.uk/churches), which I earnestly recommend. There are tasks applicable to most churches that may be irrelevant to one church but need to be done on a far more regular basis for one at the other extreme. The church architect should give guidance on the maintenance plan either in the QIR or as a separate request. The plan will vary according to the situation of the church, its construction and its condition.

1. **Situation.** Every church needs a tailored maintenance plan written for the particular needs of each church – there is no "one size fits all" plan available, unless it is written in such general terms that it is useless. I hope that it is quite evident that a church at sea level on a windswept harbour side in Cornwall is in a completely different environment to a church in leafy rural Northamptonshire or in urban London or in the Yorkshire Dales, even if they were of identical construction.

2. **Construction.** The construction of a church will vary according to its age, location and the propensity of the diocese for granting faculties that make major changes.

   - The age of a church is actually difficult to define, as most old churches will have been modified repeatedly over the centuries, from mediaeval times, to the Victorian age and up to modern times. In general, however, the original design will have influenced the subsequent alterations, although there are doubtless many exceptions. A more modern church will be made using cement rather than lime, which will completely change the maintenance plan.

   - The availability of building materials in the locality was a major consideration until the advent of cheap and reliable bulk transport. The difficulty and expense of transport made the use of the best materials only viable for the highest-profile buildings.

   - Regardless of how a building was originally built, some dioceses may have granted faculties for major changes, such as a stainless steel roof or cement tiles or a glazed extension. Such changes may reduce the maintenance requirement or even increase it – all such complications need to be included in the plan.

3. **Condition.** You might have inherited a building which
    has been severely neglected by your predecessors, in
    which case its condition is most likely to cause you a
    lot of work and cost a lot of money. On the other hand,
    you might have taken over a building which has been
    loved and cared for properly; in which case, give thanks
    for the predecessors who did such a good job! If you
    have any doubt about which category the building fits
    in when you look at it, a glance at the log book, QIR
    and maintenance list will soon tell you.

So, speak to the architect about a maintenance plan. Then,
after referring back to *Principles of Old Buildings* and the
last QIR, check for yourself: where is the building damp?
Are the hoppers clear or does rainwater flow down the
building? Is there missing pointing on the exterior walls?
Has cement been used on the pointing? Are any stones in
the walls losing their face or receding into the wall? Does
the roof leak? Are the drains working? Are the electrical
system and all portable appliances regularly checked? Is
the boiler checked? Do the toilets work properly? Are
there many broken or cracked window panes? Do bats
inhabit the church? Are there any obvious safety issues?
Has an asbestos survey ever been carried out? Is the
church secure?

Then, from your own assessment of the QIR and the
building itself, you might have developed an idea of the
major issues for your church, and where your priorities
should lie. In my view, as I said earlier, you should start
at the top and make sure that the church is watertight.
If it isn't watertight for any reason, you must get it fixed
without delay.

The trick with maintenance is to keep on top of it. If you let the routine things pile up, it then becomes a huge chore to find the energy to do any of it, whereas if you do a little bit often then suddenly one day you realise that there is nothing that needs doing for a couple of weeks. The same philosophy applies to minor repairs – things like a little bit of wood that needs regluing before it gets lost, or the hole in a little pane in a leaded window, or the loose floor tile. If you tackle these slowly, one by one, then the entire church develops that loved look. It's a good idea to take one issue, such as the hole in a small pane of glass, and see what else can be done by the same tradesman when he comes; once you start looking, you will probably find several more severely cracked panes as well as a lot with a single crack. In many cases, the single cracks can be left, but if a small pane has two or three cracks then it is worth replacing even though there is not yet a draught through it. By doing several of these at the same time, the cost of each will reduce and the glazier's visit will make quite a difference.

In this context, I remember getting the chancel stained glass window at Bogthornly fixed; one of the figures had a piece of elbow missing, and every time I went up for communion this hole irritated me. So a glazier came and fitted a temporary piece of plain glass for the time whilst he made the properly painted piece of coloured glass. I had also asked him to quote for a number of plain glass repairs, which he did very quickly – I am always impressed by the speed at which a skilled craftsman can work. One of the repairs was to replace a 10" x 12" pane in the middle of a large window (of about fifty similar panes) in the chancel; this particular pane was very obvious, being covered by a piece of once clear acetate held in place by sticky tape.

When the glazier had left, Darren (who was the verger's helper) and I looked at the repaired plain window. I said, 'I am so pleased to see that tape gone,' and Darren replied, 'So am I; I've been replacing that tape every year for the last fifteen years!'

Also at Bogthornly, the tower was open to the elements (there never was any glass in the large apertures), and I was in the lower tower once during a heavy rainstorm. To my consternation, I saw that there was water flowing down the inner face of the walls of this mediaeval tower. Investigation revealed that the tower's internal roof above me was covered in pigeon guano, and so the internal roof could not drain as planned, hence the overflow down the walls. The solution was (a) to get a specialist contractor in to clear the mess, and (b) to get a faculty to apply bird netting to the apertures to prevent a recurrence. Had I not been there whilst it was raining, that situation might have remained for years more, to the detriment of the tower. Whilst looking at this internal roof, we found some plywood which seemed to be part of a box. It transpired that a previous vicar had actually fitted bird boxes in the tower to encourage the little blighters to nest there. I am afraid that sentiment and old buildings rarely mix!

I have already written about an oft-mentioned maintenance action which is to go around the church with your wellingtons on, a pair of binoculars strapped round your neck and holding a large umbrella during a heavy rainstorm, so that you can check the correct operation (or otherwise) of all the rainwater goods. You might feel silly if anyone is watching, but I do recommend this check. If you can get internal access under the roof in a similar storm then that's a good check too, but do remove the wellingtons first (and hopefully you can leave the brolly behind too).

I personally have done a lot of maintenance work on three listed churches, but this is not part of the job specification for a CW. My philosophy about doing such work is that I cannot see why the church should pay for a contractor to do something when I can just as easily do it myself at little or no cost. However, I would add a word of caution: you must know your own limits, in skill, safety and legality. Hence, I never do work on gas appliances or mains electricity, but I am competent to set the heating timer, reboot the boiler, rewire a plug when a wire is loose, sand and repaint woodwork, replaster a small area with lime, or clear gutters when the roof is pretty flat with good access and a nice parapet wall for safety. If you can, I encourage you to do the same but, if you can't, then it's good if you find someone who can, or else you have to find a good set of local contractors. I do want to emphasise that such DIY talents are not an essential part of the CW job – but they can save the church a surprising amount of money if you can get them done without a contractor.

The point is that whatever condition it is in, you should plan to leave it in a better condition when you hand over to your successor, just as a vicar would want to leave the church in a spiritually better state and a treasurer would want to leave it in a better financial state. If all three of those can happen concurrently then the church really is moving well.

16

The Churchyard

Most old churches have a churchyard, and in many cases the churchyard is legally closed for burials. This often occurred in the mid 19th century when it seems that a lot of churchyards, especially in cities, were full and proving to be a health hazard. In London, this was when the large cemeteries such as Highgate and Earlsfield were established; these are publicly owned and run, and are nothing to do with the church. If the churchyard is closed for burials, it is possible to have permission to bury cremated ashes in a specified part. At Bogthornly, the vicar was caught out after admitting to burying ashes in the rose garden in the closed churchyard because he did not realise that a faculty was needed for this.

The churchyard will usually belong to the church. The diocesan registrar said to me once, 'The churchyard is consecrated; the clue is in that word, which means it is holy so it belongs to the church.' That also means that any footpath through the churchyard is not a public right of way, so you can close it if there is a need (such as building works).

At Clamcester, the local town council owns a cemetery which is next door to the church, and we often have to respond to questions which need to be directed to the town council – it is just an understandable public perspective that it belongs to the church due to its proximity. In fact, in many cases, the closed churchyard is also maintained by the local council, and the council might even have the common perception that they own the churchyard. This might just be true in some cases but, unless they can demonstrate when it was sold or given to them, I would suggest that they are probably in error with that assumption. The fact is that under the Local Government Act 1972, Section 215 (find it on http://www.legislation.gov.uk), the local council may be asked to take over the maintenance of a closed churchyard and this probably happened at some time in the past; since then, they have forgotten this and just assumed that they own it. The trouble comes when they decide to fit a new bench, or a new waste bin. Guess what? They need a faculty! The trouble is that they might go ahead and do it anyway. This happened at Clamcester when they were advised that they should not do it without permission and, after they did it anyway, they were made to pay the full costs of the faculty by the Chancellor, which is very unusual.

Just as people think the council's cemetery belongs to the church, they think that we have power over people who travel through the churchyard. I have been shouted at by an individual who said he had almost been hit by a bicycle in the churchyard, and he wanted me to enforce the "No Cycling" rule which was on the gate to the town cemetery. I pointed out to him that the sign applied to the council's land on the other side of the gateway, not ours, and in any case did he expect me to stand in the churchyard permanently, telling people off? He replied, 'Useless. I'm thinking of joining the other lot,' indicating the Roman Catholic church in the distance. I had to quell the unchristian desire to say that I'd never seen him in our church anyway!

One churchyard had been owned by the council and its forebears since the mid-19th century, and it had a small building in the corner which the council used as a store. Then they decided to let it, and the applicant wanted to use it as an off-licence, which the vicar started moaning about. I mentioned this potential use to the Diocesan Registry, and they very quickly pointed out to the Council that this use was against the covenants in the original conveyance. A councillor mentioned this on a local forum saying that "the church objected to the proposal". I replied saying that it was a legal objection which they were entitled to challenge in court if they wished but, after all, if it wasn't for the covenants like this then the council would have built flats on the churchyard by now! That got the support of the other forum members, and the councillor never responded. If you ever have any sort of similar legal issue regarding the churchyard, speak first to the Registry as they will know the legal situation and fight for it, saving you and the vicar a lot of effort.

17

Letting The Church

Extra income always seems a good idea, and letting the church for use by approved organisations is often a good idea, as it also makes the church more involved with the local community. However, it might in some circumstances be a poor idea which can cause grief and frustration, so that might have the opposite effect on the links with the local community!

The first thing is that you need a policy. Why do you want to hire it out? What sort of activity is regarded as permissible or not? What sort of organisation might be regarded as undesirable in this respect? Will regular users be allowed to keep anything on the premises? Are you going to trust people with a key, or will you need a volunteer to open and lock up? If your church is already being hired out, have there been any issues? How much will you charge? This sort of policy decision really should be agreed at the PCC in advance and then implemented from the start, as once people do an activity they will assume that, in the absence of complaint, the activity is acceptable. It is much more difficult to restrict an activity if they have been doing it for a long period already.

Then you will need to prepare a set of clear instructions (and, dare I say, rules?) for people who use the church. These should cover topics such as locking up, cleanliness, disposal of rubbish, behaviour, moving of furniture, use of the AV system, consumption of alcohol, heating and lighting, as well as clarifying responsibilities for security, health & safety, first aid and copyright. This list is not necessarily complete – you need to think of the other things in your church that could be an issue. With care, you can prepare one set of instructions which will apply both to any church members who are privileged with a key and also to hirers of the church. These instructions need to be precise and very detailed – if there is a way of misinterpreting instructions, users will find it. Don't assume that even intelligent people know which way is east or west in a church (as a vicar found out once when mentioning the damaged west window to the congregation).

In these rules/instructions, you have to make very clear the precise nature of what they are hiring and, equally, what they are not hiring. You will even need to state that the hirers do not have sole use of the church whilst they are hiring it – I would absolutely never agree to be prevented access at any time to the church for which I am responsible, especially when it is Grade I listed. You might even be fortunate enough to be able to hire different parts of your building to different groups at the same time. This has the potential for causing issues, whether with security, parking space, noise or use of the toilets.

Now, I wouldn't want to put you off the idea, but I need to tell you about a few experiences which show how difficult it can be to hire out a church – the sort of thing that makes you question whether the extra income is worth the hassle.

At Bogthornly, another church had been allowed to use the church twice a week. This was an African Pentecostal church, which should give you a clue about the style of their worship. I had no idea as to whether such use needed to be approved by the diocese, or if it had been – that fell under my definition of a question to which I did not want to know the answer. The origin of this arrangement was the previous vicar who had felt that we should share our church for free with other people who were not blessed with a building of their own. Yes, in case you missed it, I'll repeat it: they used the church "for free". Eventually, the vicar realised that there was indeed a significant marginal cost to us for heating, lighting and cleaning, and so they started paying a small rent. When it was increased to something sensible (I think, £100 per week), they complained vociferously.

Their Sunday meeting lasted from about 2pm to something like 6.30pm, and they had also been given use of the church on Friday evenings from 7pm to 10pm. Now, if you look at those times, they are really quite restrictive. The inability to use the church on a Friday evening was very frustrating when we were attracting working professionals who just couldn't make meetings of any sort during the week, and Sunday evenings were never very attractive to them. If we wanted to have a parish lunch after the morning service then we had to be finished and cleaned up before 2pm, which was quite difficult as our service usually lasted from 10.30 until 12.15. (Well, the 10.30 was a notional time as some in the congregation thought we started at 10.45, and the attendance would more than double between 10.30 and 11am. There were some days when it went on until 12.45, but I won't go into those experiences here.)

We had all sorts of issues with these hirers at Bogthornly: they often ate food in the enclosed south aisle, but many took their food into the church, even into the chancel; they used huge numbers of candles which often spilt hot wax on the carpet despite the use of a vast plastic sheet; I once removed a massive quantity of chewing gum from under the pews and subsequently proved that it reappeared on Sunday afternoons; their worship was very loud and got complaints from neighbouring houses, especially in summer; and they arrived in large four-wheel drive SUVs which made local parking difficult on Sunday afternoons to the annoyance of the local residents. Eventually, a plan to reorder the inside came to fruition, and the vicar wisely decided that their use of the church during that fifteen-week project would be impossible, and so asked them to find another permanent site to hire. They of course were upset over this; largely, one suspected, because of the additional unsubsidised expense of all the alternatives.

The south aisle rooms at Bogthornly were also used by Alcoholics Anonymous at a peppercorn rate (£10 for three hours on Thursday evenings if my memory serves me right). I think if you hire to a charity, you have to decide which ones you are going to subsidise and which should be asked to pay the sensible rate which contributes to your finances. If you don't need the income, then by all means subsidise lots of charities in this way, but make that decision consciously, not accidentally. Just be aware that a subsidised organisation never has an incentive to terminate their hire. The other issue with Alcoholics Anonymous is that they do like to remain anonymous, so effectively we could not enter our own church whilst they were there.

Subsequently, at Clamcester, we had a couple of non-profit organisations who hired the church for rehearsals and performances, possibly twelve or fifteen in a year. You might think that this sounds like the ideal activity for a church – it gets non-church people inside the church – but life is never easy.

One probable issue with an old building is that heating and access are often difficult. Clamcester currently has old radiators trying to heat a huge volume and on the north side has the main (but narrow) door which has not yet been made disability friendly; there is a separate disabled access through the door on the south side. I fully understand that if you want to bring a set of timpani or a couple of double basses into church, then the larger south door is the obvious option. However, if you open both north and south doors at the same time, there is a wind tunnel effect which basically causes the indoor temperature to fall dramatically in minutes. This is especially true if you leave the doors wide open whilst collecting large objects from your vehicle or whilst you are moving something down to the chancel. The physics of this are clear to me, but I have failed to persuade many users that if they let the temperature fall, the system does not have the capacity to raise it in the desired timescale. The people concerned then complained to us that the church was too cold for the musicians, but my explanation fell on deaf ears.

Another issue is the start time. If the church is hired on a Sunday, then be sure to leave plenty of time between the end of the last morning service and their start time – you don't want to feel rushed by the arrival of the hirers. On one occasion, we had had a Toy Service, and there was a pile of donated toys in front of the nave altar which I couldn't move into the vestry after the service because of the mass of performers present who were already putting their own stuff down in there in preparation for their rehearsal. There's also the question of how they treat the church property: one group actually unscrewed some wooden brackets in the church (why?) and then failed to replace them, leaving the crucifer with nowhere to put the processional cross on Sunday morning!

Then there's the mess people make. Often, users will fail to restore the church properly after a Saturday hire, and all too often they leave bin bags of their rubbish beside (or on top of) our full bin, despite a clear instruction to take their own rubbish away. They also have no idea about what plastic and paper is recycled, so the recycling bag always contains messy paper plates with food still attached, tea bags, the wrong plastic and so on. Presumably, their own recycling bins at home are treated in the same way.

In six years as CW at Clamcester, I got very annoyed by the number of times the lights were left on in the church, usually by hirers but occasionally by church members. I would not notice this until I was getting ready for bed, and invariably if the lights were on after 10.30pm, I knew that the users had gone home, so I would have to get dressed and go over there. It was only as I was in my last couple of months that I found a solution for this: I asked the administrator to put on the weekly list of events the telephone number for the last responsible person each day. Then, if the lights were on, I would phone up the person and get them to come back to do it. Even the threat of this has made people much more responsible. Result!

However, let me not put you off. If you do have a useable building, then it can be a great source of extra income. Just be aware that there can be pitfalls and you need somehow to retain sufficient control at all times.

18

Things I Have Disliked
Or Done Wrong

A friend caused me to think: what would I do differently if I could do it all again? Did I do things wrongly?

I don't want to give the impression that life as a CW has been a bowl of cherries, or that I have always found it easy; there have many hiccups along the way, many of which are due to my own personality and character. Since I am a different person to you, it follows quite logically that you and I will not make the same mistakes; I make my mistakes, and you will make your own!

Being honest at heart, I have to admit that the worst times have been the PCC meetings; this has been the case at every church where I have been on the PCC.

For some people, the PCC meeting appears to be the highlight of their week, and so they want to enjoy it and make the most of it. For me, it is a business meeting with a spiritual basis, but when there is an agenda of eighteen items and we have only reached Item 5 after an hour, I start to lose the will to live. Sadly, the result is that the meeting can go on too long and everyone becomes tired; an item not on the agenda is allowed to be raised, taking up twenty-five valuable minutes, and then a poor decision is made because we want to get on. This sort of thing is rarely to anyone's benefit, and emphasises how important it is to have a clear agenda coupled with good chairing of a meeting. The agenda must be realistic for the time allowed; if a substantive item not on the agenda is raised at the meeting then the answer is that it will be put on the agenda next time, and the person who raised it should to be asked circulate a brief about it before that meeting, or it should be discussed by the Standing Committee (although at one of the churches I mention, we didn't even have the legally required Standing Committee!).

At PCC meetings there has often been too much banter, with many members happy to talk among themselves or make sotto voce comments when other people are speaking; the trouble is that many people do not realise that there is a place and time for frivolity, humour or deviation from the point – they just want to say their piece, regardless. I feel it is the height of rudeness for people to laugh at some private joke at one end of the group whilst I am trying to interest them in "Churchwardens' Items". I was once unable to speak for ninety seconds after the chair called me, as there was a continuous backchat going on. I would like to smile benevolently and wait for it all to subside; I would love to be the sort of person who could exchange quick-fire humour; I would love not to be annoyed by such people and so I suppose I need a thicker skin. I know I should not get upset about that sort of thing, but it still riles me after all these years.

Now, I know that I always respond badly to criticism; what really galls me though is to be criticized in public by people who do nothing! There are always members who do very little, if they do anything at all; they do not think to tell me of an issue beforehand, but are happy to raise it publicly at a PCC meeting. "Why hasn't that light bulb been replaced? The latch on that cupboard is stiff". When this occurs I feel the bile rising inside me and I have learned over the years to suppress those feelings – to sit on my hands and bite my tongue at the same time. Sometimes I fail in this and as a result, when I then blow my top, people know. I can't say what I am feeling at the time, I just know that it needs to be said. Afterwards I don't feel good about it either and, yes, I regret saying things.

I know that I can't do much about my failing memory. I know I need to write things down at once, before I forget them, and I use the calendar on my mobile phone extensively to help me in this. I know I forget things, but I do find that people don't help; they tell me something irrelevant whilst I am on CW duty with a service starting in thirty seconds, or they ask me to pass a message to my wife – I reply: 'Please could you send her an email yourself!'

Sometimes I say the wrong thing, accidentally – it wasn't what I meant to say, it just came out wrongly. I now try very hard to think through what I want to say before I say it, but this then means that I might have missed the right point in the conversation to say it; I might then bring the conversation back just so I can say what I wanted – I know this isn't very helpful!

I would suggest that some of my issues stem from the fact that I am an intensely logical person, and so any lack of logic raises a warning flag to me. For me, if a PCC is to work properly, or if a CW is to do his job well, then there has to be a visible level of logical process in what is being done, especially when it comes to works on the church building. Sometimes I can clearly see the issues, the process and the resolution, and I do get agitated by people who cannot see with the same clarity but will not accept my proposed solution. Actually, although I have always been a logical person who liked to put things in order, I never thought that I was "process-driven" until, many years ago, I did a Master's degree in Business Administration. In that, I learned the benefits of "process" and, in fact, I then saw why my time in the RAF had, at times, felt quite unsatisfactory: many so-called processes were in fact not really processes at all and would have benefitted from a decent bit of business analysis to make them work logically and smoothly. You can perhaps imagine how frustrating the process-less approach was to a most logical person.

I suppose that being seen as an ultra-logical person with a strong process base and a high level of attention to detail, it is hardly surprising that there is a measurable level of OCD in what I do. I like to do things right, and I like to see them done correctly. If there is a home for something then it should be put back there, not left lying around (although I am sure that my wife would disagree in respect of my stuff around the house). So at church I am really annoyed by the people who put the wrong things in the wrong recycling bin, or don't put the AV equipment away properly, or generally think that there is storage space for a load of unsold stuff left from the last coffee morning, or put on all the lights in church because they can't be bothered to select just the set they need. Then there are the AV operators who move to the next slide a fraction late, or forget to move it on at all, or don't turn on a microphone until after someone has started speaking; and there are the people who insist that they have some sort of right to park on the wet churchyard grass in winter, regardless of the ploughed furrows that they leave behind. You get the picture?

I do try very hard not to be directly critical at all – I often fail and wish I hadn't said something which was unmerited or just too blunt; so I try to be just slightly critical in a gentle fashion, by trying to point out how to improve things whilst not directly criticising – I like to think I have become better at this, but I know there is still much room for improvement. I know that I too fail to be perfect when I operate the AV, and I chastise myself for each error, however small.

But if you stop and think, perhaps I might have a point? I would like to think that we as Christians have a duty to care for the planet by recycling as much as we can, and by not wasting carbon-fuel electricity (quite apart from not wasting the church's money). Our worship is meant to be orderly and fit for purpose, and I think that shoddy worship is an affront to God. In the same way, an untidy church or a muddy churchyard are not likely to help attract newcomers.

In fact, I think that I register slightly on the autistic scale and, occasionally, I seem to demonstrate some worrying symptoms in terms of how I express myself. Recently, I have also discovered online a thing called "aphantasia", which is a term that describes people who cannot see things with their "mind's eye". It's not an illness but rather just a different situation, comparable to being left-handed;

in fact, I don't really know what others mean by their "mind's eye" – I cannot imagine a picture; I can only recall an image of something I have seen. I think this explains why I have always had trouble with understanding poetry or art and, equally, why I have difficulty in worship – I rarely feel that I have reached out to God in a church service.

But, I argue, these are all part of me. They describe the "me" that God created and I wouldn't want to try to change that. Consequently, I cannot accept that some apparently wrong things which I have done are actually wrong; I have just done them in a different way to how other people would like to see them done.

19

Things I Have Done Right

No, I am not going to boast of my achievements as CW; I would not even like to think of starting to list the things I have done at the church over the years. It's not that I am really modest, as I confess that I do like my efforts to be acknowledged – I am human after all. I have been praised as being an "outstanding CW" and "one of my best CWs", and I know that my efforts are generally much appreciated inasmuch as other people have seen them. I have done many things which most people have never noticed, as they take it for granted that these things get done somehow. The things that I have done right are essentially the things that I decided long ago were my aims and motivations in the role; they have been mentioned separately earlier, but I want to repeat them in conclusion:

Firstly, in talking about the church buildings earlier, I suggested that *your aim as CW should be to pass on to your successor, when you finish your term, a church building which is measurably better than the one you took over*. I believe that I have achieved that as CW in two different churches, and so I take inward satisfaction from that.

Secondly, I said that as CW I should be helping the vicar to do her job more effectively, by taking away from her as many as possible of the tasks that she doesn't need to do personally. I have tried to do this and have been generally successful in doing in her place some of the things which are perhaps boring and ordinary; therefore, I sincerely believe that I have played my part in the Kingdom.

Finally, I have already quoted my favourite verse which is Matthew ch 5, v 16: *Let your light so shine before men [and women] that they may see your good works and give glory to your Father in heaven.* Everything that I have done was done for that reason. I know that I am already saved through grace, and I can do nothing to improve on that. Fundamentally, I am not after the gratitude of men and women, because I know that God sees what I do and that is enough for me.

If you are a CW, or are thinking of becoming one, I commend these motivations to you.

A

Glossary – Terminology Of Old Buildings

I realise that I ought to explain a few terms which are pretty common in respect of old buildings. Not all churches will have all of these features, but most are applicable to many churches as well as other old buildings.

Coping – the piece of angled stone which is often placed on top of a wall to enable the water to run off. The edge is meant to be carefully shaped to make this happen; and if it is worn away, you might find that the water runs down the wall instead, which will cause damage to the wall.

Corbel – a piece of stone which is set into a wall and juts out so that it can support another stone or (internally) a wooden ceiling joist, etc.

Finial – if you have ever fitted a modern curtain rail, you might well have fitted a finial at either end. On a church, the finial is the (probably decorative) bit on top of a pinnacle.

Gable – a wall at the end of a building (e.g., a chancel) where two sloping roofs meet at a ridge.

Hood moulding – the arched piece of stone above a window or doorway, usually following the line of the window. This is to stop any water flowing down the wall onto the door or window beneath.

Hopper – the receptacle where flowing water from a gutter is funnelled into the downpipe. These may be made of lead if they are old, and may often be decorated and have the year of manufacture cast into the face – look after these!

Joists – the horizontal timbers supporting a floor or ceiling.

Lancet – the narrow window typically used to give light to spiral staircases.

Lath – thin strips of wood in a wall or ceiling, carefully laid a small distance apart, so that plaster can be spread over. When done properly, this gives the impression of a set of little waves of plaster getting pushed through the lath (on the side you can't normally see); these are called the nibs and are how the plaster is held to the ceiling. (NB The word is "lath", not "lathe", which is a very different thing entirely!)

Lintel – a horizontal structural piece (stone or wood) which supports the wall above a door or window.

Merlon – a church tower or parapet wall might well have a notched effect with equally spaced higher and lower parts; these are often termed the "battlements" for want of a better word. The bit which stands above is called the merlon.

Mullion – A vertical member, in wood or stone, dividing a window or other opening into individual lights.

Perpendicular joints (sometimes abbreviated to "perpend joints") – in a string course, these are prone to erosion if water has been allowed to flow down the wall. You can see where this has happened because there will probably be discolouration beneath where the joint has failed and allowed water to run through.

Pinnacle – one of the vertical pointed things which often occur on churches with a tower – the tower is usually square and there will probably be a pinnacle at each corner.

Purlin – a horizontal length of wood in the structure of a pitched roof, about halfway up the angle of the truss, which joins the trusses together. This is very important for the strength of the roof.

Quoin – the smoothly faced stones on the corners of stone structures, which give strength to the corner.

Rafters – the angled timbers in a roof structure.

Sarking – a covering of boards over the roof trusses, essential under a lead roof covering but which can also be laid under a pitched slate roof under the battens.

String course, or drip course – the horizontal line of stone which is fitted into an external wall so that any water which goes down the wall is then enabled to drip off the wall; if it is worn away you might find that the water runs down the wall instead, which ultimately will damage the lime mortar and possibly the internal plaster.

Verdigris – a green or bluish deposit especially of copper carbonates, formed on copper, brass, or bronze surfaces by exposure to air or seawater over a period of time. May also be present on stone underneath these metals.

B

Abbreviations
As Used In This Book

ACW – Assistant Churchwarden
APCM – Annual Parochial Church Meeting
AV – Audio Visual
CC – Charity Commission
C of E – Church of England
CW – Churchwarden
DAC – Diocesan Advisory Committee
DPC – Damp proof course
GASDS – Gift Aid Small Donations Scheme
LLM – Licensed Lay Minister
LPWGS – Listed Places of Worship Grant Scheme
PCC – Parochial Church Council
PTO – Permission to Officiate
QI – Quinquennial Inspection
QIR – Quinquennial Inspection Report
SSM – Self-Supporting Minister
The Rules – The Charities Act 2011 and the PCC (5th Edition, 2017)
TRIO – "The Responsibility Is Ours"

C

Index